GUI Design for Android Apps

T0219531

Ryan Cohen, Lead Project Editor
Tao Wang, Lead Contributing Author

GUI Design for Android Apps

Ryan Cohen & Tao Wang

Publisher: Heinz Weinheimer
Associate Publisher: Jeffrey Pepper
Lead Editors: Steve Weiss (Apress); Stuart Douglas and Paul Cohen (Intel)
Coordinating Editor: Melissa Maldonado
Cover Designer: Anna Ishchenko

Distributed to the book trade worldwide by Springer Science+Business Media New York, 233 Spring Street, 6th Floor, New York, NY 10013. Phone 1-800-SPRINGER, fax (201) 348-4505, e-mail orders-ny@springer-sbm.com, or visit www.springeronline.com.

For information on translations, please e-mail rights@apress.com, or visit www.apress.com.

About ApressOpen

What Is ApressOpen?

- ApressOpen is an open access book program that publishes high-quality technical and business information.

- ApressOpen eBooks are available for global, free, noncommercial use.

- ApressOpen eBooks are available in PDF, ePub, and Mobi formats.

- The user-friendly ApressOpen free eBook license is presented on the copyright page of this book.

Contents at a Glance

Contents

About the Lead Project Editor

Ryan Cohen is the contributing editor responsible for leading the international team of content contributors who created this Intel learning resource; he's also an Android enthusiast and Portland State graduate. Ryan has been following Android since 2011 when he made the switch from Apple iOS. When he is not writing about Android, he spends his time researching anything and everything new in the world of Android.

About the Lead Contributing Author

 **Tao Wang** came to United States as a Ph.D. student to study at Oregon State University in 1993. He has been a software engineer with Intel Corporation since 2002. Tao began blogging and writing about Android in 2008; and, since 2011, he has served as a technical collateral manager for the Intel Android Developer Zone, the developer resource for all things Android at Intel. In his spare time, Tao also runs his own mobile app/client education startup called E-k12. He follows closely the latest progress in application development, as well as testing/debugging/performance optimization for mobile devices and Android on x86 platforms. Tao is skilled in many platforms, including Android SDK and NDK; Intel Android tools; game engines such as Cocos2D-x, AndEngine, and libgdx; OpenGL ES; RenderScript; and Android Runtime. His other areas of interest include mobile Internet technologies such as online content management, cloud-based mobile technologies, embedded devices, robotics, and mobile learning on the go.

About the Technical Reviewer

Xavier Hallade is Developer Evangelist for the Intel Software and Services Group in Paris, France. Since 2012 and the public release of the first Android smartphone based on an Intel platform, he has been helping Android developers improve their support for new hardware and technologies made or supported by Intel.

Introduction

This mini book is a collection of four chapters pulled from *Android Application Development for the Intel Platform*, designed to give developers an introduction to creating great user interfaces for their Android applications. These chapters cover topics ranging from the differences between developing UIs for desktop systems and embedded systems to optimizing the UI of applications for touchscreens.

Chapter 1

This chapter introduces the general GUI design method for desktop systems and then shows how designing the UI and UX for embedded systems is different. Next, it discusses general methods and principles of GUI design for Android applications and how to develop user interfaces suitable for typical user interaction on Android smartphone and tablets.

Chapter 2

This chapter introduces Android interface design by having you create a simple application called GuiExam. You learn about the state transitions of activities, the Context class, intents, and the relationship between applications and activities. Finally, the chapter shows how to use the layout as an interface by changing the layout file activity_main.xml, and how the button, event, and inner event listeners work.

Chapter 3

In this chapter, you learn how to create an application with multiple activities. This application is used to introduce the explicit and implicit trigger mechanisms of activities. Next, you see an example of an application with parameters triggered by an activity in a different application, which will help you understand of the exchange mechanism for the activity's parameters.

Chapter 4

This chapter introduces the basic framework of drawing in the view, how the drawing framework responds to touchscreen input, and how to control the display of the view as well as the multi-touch code framework. Examples illustrate the multi-touch programming framework and keyboard-input responses. You also learn how to respond to hardware buttons on Android devices, such as Volume +, Volume -, Power, Home, Menu, Back, and Search. After that, you see the three different dialog boxes for Android, including the activity dialog theme, specific dialog classes, and toast reminders. Finally, you learn how to change application property settings.

■ ■ ■

CHAPTER 1

GUI Design for Android Apps, Part 1: General Overview

Since its emergence in the 1980s, the concept of the *graphical user interface* (GUI) has become an indispensable part of *human-computer interaction* (HCI). As embedded systems have evolved, they have gradually adopted this concept as well. The Android embedded OS running on the Intel Atom hardware platform is at the forefront of this movement.

Because resources are limited, the GUI design of Android systems is more challenging than that of desktop systems. In addition, users have more rigorous demands and expectations for a high-quality user experience. Interface design has become one of the important factors in determining the success of systems and applications on the market. This chapter introduces how to develop user interfaces suitable for typical user interaction on Android embedded systems.

Overview of GUIs for Embedded Applications

These days, the user interface (UI) and user experience (UX) of software are increasingly important factors in determining whether software will be accepted by users and achieve market success. UX designs are based on the types of input/output or interaction devices and must comply with their characteristics. Compared to desktop computer systems, Android systems have different interaction devices and modalities. If a desktop's UI designs are copied indiscriminately, an Android device will present a terrible UI and unbearable UX, unacceptable to users. In addition, with greater expectations for compelling user experiences, developers must be more meticulous and careful in designing system UIs and UXs, making them comply with the characteristics of embedded applications.

This chapter first introduces the general GUI design method for desktop systems and then shows how designing UIs for embedded systems is different. The aim is to help you quickly master general methods and principles of GUI design for Android applications.

Characteristics of Interaction Modalities of Android Devices

A general-purpose desktop computer has powerful input/output (or interaction) devices such as a large, high-resolution screen, a full keyboard and mouse, and diverse interaction modalities. Typical desktop computer screens are at least 17 inches, with resolutions of at least 1,280 × 960 pixels. The keyboard is generally a full keyboard or an enhanced keyboard. On full keyboards, letters, numbers, and other characters are located on corresponding keys—that is, full keyboards provide keys corresponding to all characters. Enhanced keyboards have additional keys. The distance between keys on a full keyboard is about 19 mm, which is convenient for users to make selections.

The GUI interactive mode of desktop computers based on screen, keyboard, and mouse is referred to as WIMP (windows, icons, menus, and pointers), which is a style of GUI using these elements as well as interactive elements including buttons, toolbars, and dialog boxes. WIMP depends on screen, keyboard, and mouse devices to complete the interaction. For example, a mouse (or a device similar to a mouse, such as a light pen) is used for pointing, a keyboard is used to input characters, and a screen shows the output.

In addition to screens, keyboards, mice, and other standard interaction hardware, desktop computers can be equipped with joysticks, helmets, data gloves, and other multimedia interactive devices to achieve multimedia computing functions. By installing cameras, microphones, speakers, and other devices, and by virtue of their powerful computing capabilities, users can interact with desktop computers in the form of voice, gestures, facial expressions, and other modalities.

Desktop computers are also generally equipped with CD-ROM/DVDs and other large-capacity portable external storage devices. With these external storage devices, desktop computers can release software and verify ownership and certificates through CD/DVD.

As a result of the embeddability and limited resources of embedded systems, as well as user demand for portability and mobility, Android systems have interaction modalities, methods, and capabilities that are distinct from those of desktop systems. Due to these characteristics and conditions, interaction on Android systems is more demanding and more difficult to achieve than it is on desktop systems.

The main differences between Android devices and desktop computers are described next.

Screens of Various Sizes, Densities, and Specifications

Instead of large, high-resolution screens like those on desktop computers, Android device screens are smaller and have various dimensions and densities measured in dots per inch (DPI). For example, the K900 smartphone's screen is 5.5 inches with a resolution of 1920 ×1080 pixels, and some smartphone screens are only 3.2 inches.

The aspect ratio of Android device screens is not the conventional aspect ration of 16:9 or 4:3 used by desktop computers. If Android devices adopted the interaction mode of desktop computers, many problems would result, such as a blurry display and errors in selecting targets.

Keypads and Special Keys

Desktop computers have full keyboards, where a key corresponds to every character and the generous distance between keys makes typing convenient. If an Android device has a keyboard, it's usually a keypad instead of the full keyboard. Keypads have fewer keys than full keyboards; several characters generally share one key. A keypad's keys are smaller and more tightly spaced than on full keyboards, making it harder to select and type characters. As a result, keypads are less convenient to use than full keyboards. In addition, some keypads provide special keys that are not found on standard full keyboards, so users must adjust their input on the Android device.

Generally speaking, on Android devices, keys and buttons are a unified concept. Whether you press a button or a key, the action is processed as a keyboard event with a uniform numbering scheme. Keyboard events in Android have corresponding android.view.KeyEvent classes. Figure 1-1's button/key callouts correspond to the event information listed in Table 1-1.

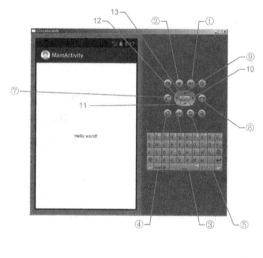

(a) Lenovo Phone K900   (b) Emulator

Figure 1-1. Keyboard and buttons of an Android phone

3

Table 1-1. *Android Event Information Corresponding to Key and Button Events*

Key/Button	Key Code	Another Name	Key Event
Key ① in Figure 1-1	24	KEYCODE_VOLUME_UP	{action=0 code=24 repeat=0 meta=0 scancode=115 mFlags=8}
Key ② in Figure 1-1	25	KEYCODE_VOLUME_DOWN	{action=0 code=25 repeat=0 meta=0 scancode=114 mFlags=8}
Key ③ in Figure 1-1	82	KEYCODE_MENU	{action=0 code=82 repeat=0 meta=0 scancode=139 mFlags=8}
Key ④ in Figure 1-1	No response		
Key ⑤ in Figure 1-1	4	KEYCODE_BACK	{action=0 code=4 repeat=0 meta=0 scancode=158 mFlags=8}
Key ⑥ in Figure 1-1	No response		
A–Z	29–54	KEYCODE_A–KEYCODE_Z	
0–9	7–16	KEYCODE_0–KEYCODE_9	
Key ⑨ in Figure 1-1	19	KEYCODE_DPAD_UP	
Key 11 in Figure 1-1	20	KEYCODE_DPAD_DOWN	
Key 12 in Figure 1-1	21	KEYCODE_DPAD_LEFT	
Key 10 in Figure 1-1	22	KEYCODE_DPAD_RIGHT	{ action=ACTION_DOWN, keyCode=KEYCODE_DPAD_RIGHT, scanCode=106, metaState=0, flags=0x8, repeatCount=0, eventTime=254791, downTime=254791, deviceId=0, source=0x301 }

(continued)

4

Table 1-1. *(continued)*

Key/Button	Key Code	Another Name	Key Event
Key 13 in Figure 1-1	23	KEYCODE_DPAD_CENTER	{ action=ACTION_DOWN, keyCode=KEYCODE_DPAD_CENTER, scanCode=232, metaState=0, flags=0x8, repeatCount=0, eventTime=321157, downTime=321157, deviceId=0, source=0x301 }
Key ⑦ in .Figure 1-1	5	KEYCODE_CALL	{ action=ACTION_DOWN, keyCode=KEYCODE_CALL, scanCode=231, metaState=0, flags=0x8, repeatCount=0, eventTime=331714, downTime=331714, deviceId=0, source=0x301 }
Key ⑧ in Figure 1-1	6	KEYCODE_ENDCALL	

See help documents like that for android.view.KeyEvent for details. Table 1-1's contents are excerpts.

Touch Screens and Styluses, in Place of Mice

A *touch screen* is an input device covering a display device to record touch positions. By using the touch screen, users can have a more intuitive reaction to the information displayed. Touch screens are widely applied to Android devices and replace a mouse for user input. The most common types of touch screens are resistive touch screens, capacitive touch screens, surface acoustic wave touch screens, and infrared touch screens, with resistive and capacitive touch screens being most often applied to Android devices. Users can directly click videos and images on the screen to watch them.

A stylus can be used to perform functions similar to touch. Some styluses are auxiliary tools for touch screens and replace fingers, helping users complete elaborate pointing, selecting, line drawing, and other operations, especially when the touch screen is small. Other styluses implement touch and input functions along with other system components. With the first type of auxiliary tool styluses, users can touch and input characters with fingers. But the second type of stylus is an indispensable input tool and is used instead of fingers.

Touch and styluses can perform most functions that mice typically do, such as click and drag, but can't achieve all the functions of mice, such as right-click and left-click/right-click at the same time. When designing embedded applications, you should control the interaction mode within the range of functions that touch screens or styluses can provide and avoid operations that are not available.

Onscreen Keyboards

Onscreen keyboards, also known as *virtual keyboards* or *soft keyboards*, are displayed on the screen via software. Users tap the virtual keys like they would tap the keys on physical keyboards.

Few Multimodal Interactions

Multimodal interaction refers to human-computer interaction with the modes involving the five human senses. It allows the user to interact through input modalities such as speech, handwriting, and hand gesture. Because computing capability is limited, Android devices generally do not adopt multimodal interaction.

Few Large-Capacity Portable External Storage Devices

Most Android devices do not have the CD-ROM/DVD drives, hard disks, or other large-capacity portable storage peripherals such as solid-state drives (SSDs) that are usually configured on desktop computers. These devices cannot be used on Android devices to install software or verify ownership and certificates. However, Android devices usually support microSD cards, which now have capacities of up to 128 GB; and more and more cloud-based storage solutions such as Dropbox, One Drive, and Google Drive are being developed for Android devices, with Android-compatible client apps available for download from Google Play Store.

UI Design Principles for Embedded Systems

This section introduces interactive design issues and corrective measures to take when transforming traditional desktop applications to embedded applications.

Considerations of Screen Size

Compared to desktop computer systems, Android systems have smaller screens with different display densities and aspect ratios. Such screen differences result in many problems when migrating applications from desktop systems to Android systems. If developers reduce desktop system screens proportionally, the graphic elements become too small to be seen clearly. In particular, it is often difficult to see the text and icons, select and click some buttons, and place some application pictures on the screen appropriately. If developers migrate application graphic elements to Android systems without changing their sizes, the screen space is limited and can only accommodate a few of the graphic elements.

Size of Text and Icons

Another problem is the size of text and icons. When an application is reduced from a typical 15-inch desktop screen to a typical 5- or 7-inch phone or tablet screen, its text is too small to be seen clearly. In addition to the size of the text font, the text window (such as a chat window) also becomes too small to read the text. Trying to reduce the font size to suit smaller windows makes the text hard to recognize.

Therefore, the design of embedded systems should use as few text prompt messages as possible; for example, replace the text with graphic or sound information. In addition, where text is necessary, the text size should be adjustable. On Android, some predefined fonts and icons are available in the res directory, such as drawable-hdpi, drawable-mdpi, and drawable-xhdpi.

Clickability of Buttons and Other Graphical Elements

Similar to the problem of small text, buttons and other graphical elements also bring interaction problems when migrating applications. On desktop systems, the size of buttons is designed for mouse clicks, whereas on Android systems, the button size should be suitable for fingers (on touch screens) or styluses. Therefore, when porting a Windows-based app to support Android devices, the application UI needs to be redesigned; and predefined drawables provided by the Android SDK should be selected in order to suit fingers or styluses.

Developers should use bigger and clearer buttons or graphic elements to avoid such problems and leave enough gap between graphic elements to avoid errors, which are common when a small touch screen is used for selecting by fingers or styluses. In addition, if an application has text labels near buttons, the labels should be part of the clickable area connected with the buttons, so the buttons are easier to click.

Size of Application Windows

Many applications, such as games, use windows with fixed sizes instead of windows that automatically adjust to fill any size screen. When these applications are migrated to Android systems, because the screen's aspect ratio does not match its resolution, part of the picture may not be seen, or part of the area may not be reachable.

These problems may be more complicated on smartphones and tablets because their screens have various densities such as small (426 dp × 320 dp), normal (470 dp × 320 dp), large (640 dp × 480 dp), and extra large (960 dp × 720 dp). Their aspect ratios are diverse and different from those commonly adopted by desktop systems.

One good way to solve such problems is to place the entire application window proportionally on the smartphone or tablet screen, such as the large and extra-large screens, which are typically 640 × 480 pixels and 960 × 720 pixels; or rearrange the UI to make full use of the entire widescreen area; or make the entire app window a scrollable view. In addition, you can allow users to use multiple touch fingers touch to zoom in, zoom out, or move the application window on the screen.

Considerations Arising from Touch Screens and Styluses

As mentioned earlier, touch screens and styluses are used on many Android systems to perform some traditional mouse functions. Such input devices are called *tap-only touch screens*. However, tap-only touch screens cannot provide all mouse functions. There is no right button, and the current finger/stylus location cannot be captured when the screen is not touched. So, desktop applications that allow functions such as cursor moves without clicking, different operations for left-clicks and right-clicks, and so on, cannot be realized on Android systems using touch screens and styluses.

The following sections talk about several problems often seen when migrating applications from desktop systems to Android systems using tap-only touch screens.

Correctly Interpreting the Movement and Input of the Cursor (Mouse) on Tap-Only Touch Screens

Many applications need mouse movement information when no mouse key is pressed. This operation is called *moving the cursor without clicking*. For example, a lot of PC shooting games[1] simulate the user's field of vision such that moving the mouse without clicking is interpreted as moving the game player's vision field; but the cursor should always stay in the middle of the new vision field. However, an embedded device with a tap-only touch screen does not support the operation of moving the cursor without clicking. Once the user's finger touches the screen, a tap event is triggered. When the user moves a finger on the screen, a series of tap events at different positions is triggered; these events are interpreted by the existing game code as additional interaction events (that is, moving the aiming position of the game player's gun).

The original interaction mode needs to be modified when migrating this type of application to Android systems. For example, this problem can be modified into a click operation: once the user touches the screen, the game screen should immediately switch to the vision field, in which the cursor is located at the screen center. This way, the cursor is always displayed at the screen center and not at the position the user actually touched. One advantage you benefit from on mobile platforms is that most smartphones and tablets on the market are equipped with sensors such as accelerometers, gyroscopes, GPS sensors, and compasses, and they allow applications to read data from the sensors. As a result, developers have more options than just touch input.

More generally, if an application needs to track the cursor's movement from point A to point B, the tap-only touch screen can define this input by the user clicking first point A and then point B, without the need to track the movement between point A and point B.

---

[1]A typical example is the game Counter-Strike (CS).

Setting Screen Mapping Correctly

Many applications run in full-screen mode. If such applications do not perfectly fill the entire tap-only touch screen (that is, they are smaller or bigger than the screen), input mapping errors result: there is a deviation between the display position and the click position.

One situation that often occurs in migrating a full-screen application to a tap-only touch screen with a low aspect ratio is the application window being centered on the screen with blank space showing on both sides. For example, when a desktop application window with a resolution of 640 × 480 (or 800 × 600) pixels is migrated to a tap-only touch screen with a resolution of 960 × 720 (or 1280 × 800, a WXGA on Dell Venue 8) pixels, it appears on the screen as shown in Figure 1-2. The resulting mapping errors cause the app to incorrectly respond to user interaction. When the user taps the position of the yellow arrow (the target), the position identified by the application is the point where the red explosion icon is located. These kinds of errors also occur when the user taps a button.

Figure 1-2. *Screen-mapping errors due to a low aspect ratio*

You should consider the position-mapping logic and take this blank space into consideration, even if the blank space is not part of the migrating application's window. By making these changes, the tap-only touch screen can map the touch position correctly.

Another situation occurs when the desktop full-screen window is migrated to a tap-only touch screen with a higher aspect ratio. The height of the original application window does not fit on the tap-only touch screen, and mapping errors occur in the vertical direction instead of the horizontal direction.

Figure 1-3 shows the original application window filling the screen horizontally but not vertically on a tap-only touch screen with a higher aspect ratio. Here, when the user taps the position of the yellow arrow (the target), the position identified by the application is the point where the red explosion icon is located. These errors are caused by the difference in shape between the physical display and the application window.

Figure 1-3. Screen-mapping errors due to a high aspect ratio

One solution is to ensure that the OS accurately maps the tap-only touch screen to the entire visible area of the screen. The OS provides special services to complete the screen stretching and mouse position mapping. Another solution is to consider, at the beginning of application development, allowing configuration options to support preconfigured display densities and aspect ratios provided by the Android SDK, such as screens with a resolution of 640 × 480, 960 × 720, or 1,080 × 800 pixels. This way, if the final dimension deformation is acceptable, the application may automatically stretch the window to cover the whole screen.

How to Solve Hover-Over Problems

Many applications allow hover-over operations: that is, users can place the mouse over a certain object or locate the mouse over an application icon to trigger an animated item or display a tooltip. This operation is commonly used to provide instructions for new players in games; but it is not compatible with the characteristics of tap-only touch screens, because they do not support the mouse hover-over operation.

You should consider selecting an alternative event to trigger animations or tips. For example, when the user touches the operation of applications, relevant animated themes and tips are triggered automatically. Another method is to design an interface interaction mode that temporarily interprets tap events as mouse hover-over events. For example, the action of pressing a certain button and moving the cursor would not be interpreted as a tap operation.

Providing Right-Click Functionality

As mentioned before, tap-only touch screens generally do not support right-click operations on mice. A commonly used alternative is a delayed touch (much longer than the tap time) to represent a right-click. This could result in the wrong operation occurring if the user accidentally releases their finger too soon. In addition, this method cannot perform simultaneous left-click and right-click (also known as *double-click*).

You should provide a user-interaction interface that can replace the right-click function: for example, using double-click or installing a clickable control on the screen to replace the right-click.

Keyboard Input Problems

As mentioned earlier, desktop computers use full keyboards, whereas Android systems usually have much simpler keypads, button panels, user-programmable buttons, and a limited number of other input devices. These limitations cause some problems when designing embedded applications that are not seen in desktop systems.

Restricting the Input of Various Commands

The keyboard limitations on Android systems make it difficult for users to type a large number of characters. Therefore, applications that require users to input many characters, especially those depending on command input, need appropriate adjustments when migrating to an Android system.

One solution is to provide an input mode that restricts the number of characters by reducing the number of commands or selectively using convenient tools like menu item shortcut keys. A more flexible solution is to create command buttons on the screen, especially context-sensitive buttons (that is, buttons that appear only when needed).

Meeting Keyboard Demand

Applications need keyboard input, such as naming a file, creating personal data, saving progress, and supporting online chat. Most applications tend to use the screen keyboard to input characters, but the screen keyboard does not always run or show at the front of the application interface, making character-input problems hard to solve.

One solution is to either design a mode without explicit conflict with the onscreen keyboard application (for example, not using the full-screen default operation mode) for applications, or provide an onscreen keyboard in the UI that appears only when needed. Another simple way of minimizing keyboard input is to provide default text string values, such as default names of personal data and default names of saved files, and allow users to select by touching. To obtain other information required by the text string (for example, prefix and suffix of file names), you can add a selection button that provides a list of character strings you've established, from which the user can select. The name of a saved file can also be uniquely obtained by combining various user information items extracted from the screen or even using the date-time stamp. Some text input services (such as a chat service) should be disabled if they are not the core functions of an application. This will not cause any negative impact on the user experience.

Software Distribution and Copyright Protection Problems

Desktop computers are generally equipped with CD-ROM/DVD drives, and their software is generally distributed via CD/DVD. In addition, for anti-piracy purposes, CD/DVD installation usually requires users to verify the ownership of the disk or load contents dynamically from the CD/DVD, especially video files. However, Android systems (smartphones and tablets, for instance) generally do not have CD-ROM/DVD drives; Android does support an external microSD card, but directly installing an application from it is still not supported.

A good solution is to allow users to download or install applications via the Internet instead of installing from CD/DVD. Consumers buy and install applications directly from application stores such as the Apple App store, Google Play, and Amazon Appstore. This popular software release model allows mobile developers to use certificates, online accounts, or other software-based ways to verify ownership, instead of physical CD/DVDs. Similarly, you should consider providing the option of placing content on an online cloud service instead of requiring users to download videos and other content from a CD/DVD.

Android Application Overview

The following sections describe the application file framework and component structure of Android applications.

Application File Framework

Figure 1-4 shows the file structure after the generation of the HelloAndroid app (this is an Eclipse screen shot).

Figure 1-4. *Example file structure of an Android project*

Even if you are not using Eclipse, you can directly access the project folder and see the same file structure, as listed next:

```
E:\Android Dev\workspace\HelloAndroid>TREE /F
E:.
    .classpath
    .project
    AndroidManifest.xml
    ic_launcher-web.png
    proguard-project.txt
    project.properties        .

——.settings
        org.eclipse.jdt.core.prefs

——assets
——bin
        AndroidManifest.xml
        classes.dex
        HelloAndroid.apk
        resources.ap_

    ——classes
      └—com
          └—example
              └—helloandroid
                        BuildConfig.class
                        MainActivity.class
                        R$attr.class
                        R$dimen.class
                        R$drawable.class
                        R$id.class
                        R$layout.class
                        R$menu.class
                        R$string.class
                        R$style.class
                        R.class

    └—res
        ——drawable-hdpi
                ic_action_search.png
                ic_launcher.png

        ——drawable-ldpi
                ic_launcher.png
```

```
            ├─drawable-mdpi
            │       ic_action_search.png
            │       ic_launcher.png
            │
            └─drawable-xhdpi
                    ic_action_search.png
                    ic_launcher.png
├─gen
│   └─com
│       └─example
│           └─helloandroid
│                   BuildConfig.java
│                   R.java
│
├─libs
│       android-support-v4.jar
│
├─res
│   ├─drawable-hdpi
│   │       ic_action_search.png
│   │       ic_launcher.png
│   │
│   ├─drawable-ldpi
│   │       ic_launcher.png
│   │
│   ├─drawable-mdpi
│   │       ic_action_search.png
│   │       ic_launcher.png
│   │
│   ├─drawable-xhdpi
│   │       ic_action_search.png
│   │       ic_launcher.png
│   │
│   ├─layout
│   │       activity_main.xml
│   │
│   ├─menu
│   │       activity_main.xml
│   │
│   ├─values
│   │       dimens.xml
│   │       strings.xml
│   │       styles.xml
```

```
├─values-large
│       dimens.xml
│
├─values-v11
│       styles.xml
│
└─values-v14
        styles.xml
└─src
  └─com
     └─example
        └─helloandroid
               MainActivity.java
```

Let's explain the features of this Android project file structure:

- src *directory*: Contains all source files.

- R.java *file*: Is automatically generated by the Android SDK integrated in Eclipse. You do not need to modify its contents.

- *Android library*: A set of Java libraries used by Android applications.

- assets *directory*: Stores mostly multimedia files and other files.

- res *directory*: Stores preconfigured resource files such as drawable layouts used by applications.

- values *directory*: Stores mostly strings.xml, colors.xml, and arrays.xml.

- AndroidManifest.xml: Equivalent to an application configuration file. Contains the application's name, activity, services, providers, receivers, permissions, and so on.

- drawable *directory*: Stores mostly image resources used by applications.

- layout *directory*: Stores mostly layout files used by applications. These layout files are XML files.

Similar to general Java projects, a src folder contains all the .java files for a project; and a res folder contains all the project resources, such as application icons (drawable), layout files, and constant values.

The next sections introduce the AndroidManifest.xml file, a must-have of every Android project, and the R.java file in the gen folder, which is included in other Java projects.

AndroidManifest.xml

The AndroidManifest.xml file contains information about your app essential to the Android system, which the system must have before it can run any of the app's code. This information includes activities, services, permissions, providers, and receivers used in the project. An example is shown in Figure 1-5.

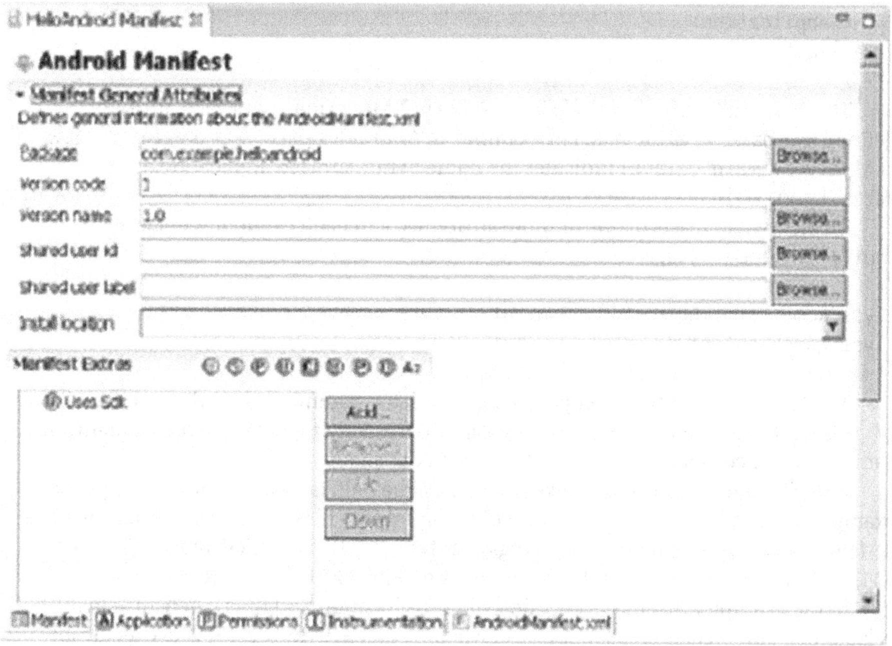

Figure 1-5. *The content of* AndroidManifest.xml *displayed in Eclipse*

The file's code is as follows:

```
<manifest xmlns:android="http://schemas.android.com/apk/res/android"
    package="com.example.helloandroid"
    android:versionCode="1"
    android:versionName="1.0" >
    <uses-sdk
        android:minSdkVersion="8"
        android:targetSdkVersion="15" />
    <application
        android:icon="@drawable/ic_launcher"
        android:label="@string/app_name"
        android:theme="@style/AppTheme" >
```

```
    <activity
        android:name=".MyMainActivity"
        android:label="@string/title_activity_my_main" >
        <intent-filter>
            <action android:name="android.intent.action.MAIN" />
            <category android:name="android.intent.category.LAUNCHER" />
        </intent-filter>
    </activity>
  </application>
</manifest>
```

The AndroidManifest.xml file is a text file in XML format, with each attribute defined by a name = value pair. For example, in Android, label = "@ string / title_activity_my_main", label indicates the name of the Android application as activity_my_main.

An element consists of one or more attributes, and each element is enclosed by the start (<) and end (/>) tags:

```
<Type Name [attribute set]> Content </ type name>
<Type Name Content />
```

The format [attribute set] can be omitted; for example, the <intent-filter> ... </ intent-filter> text segment corresponds to the activity content of the element, and <action... />corresponds to the action element.

XML elements are nested in layers to indicate their affiliation, as shown in the previous example. The action element is nested within the intent-filter element, which illustrates certain aspects of the properties or settings of intent-filter. Detailed information about XML is beyond the scope of this book, but many excellent XML books are available.

In the example, intent-filter describes the location and time when an activity is launched and creates an intent object whenever an activity (or OS) is to execute an operation. The information carried by the intent object can describe what you want to do, which data and type of data you want to process, and other information. Android compares the intent-filter data exposed by each application and finds the most suitable activity to handle the data and operations specified by the caller.

Descriptions for the main attribute entries in the AndroidManifest.xml file are listed in Table 1-2.

Table 1-2. The Main Attribute Entries in the AndroidManifest.xml File

Parameter	Description
Manifest	Root node that contains all contents in the package.
xmlns:android	Contains the manifest of the namespace.
	xmlns:android=http://schemas.android.com/apk/res/android. Makes various standard properties usable in the file and provides data to most elements.

(continued)

18

Table 1-1. *(continued)*

Parameter	Description
package	Package of manifest application.
Application	Contains the root node of the application-level component manifest in the package. This element can also contain some global and default properties for the application, such as label, icon, theme, and necessary permissions. One manifest may contain zero or one (no more than one) element.
android:icon	Icon of the application.
android:label	Name of the application.
Activity	Name of the initial page to load when users start the application. It is an important tool for user interaction. Most other pages are displayed when other activities are performed or manifested by other activity flags. Note: Each activity must have a corresponding <activity> flag whether it is used externally or in its own package. If an activity has no corresponding flag, you cannot operate it. In addition, to support a searching activity, an activity can contain one or several <intent-filter> elements to describe the operations it supports.
android:name	Default activity launched by the application.
intent-filter	Is formed by manifesting the intent value supported by a designated component. In addition to specifying different types of values, intent-filter can specify properties for describing a unique label, icon, or other information required by an operation.
Action	Intent action supported by a component.
Category	Intent category supported by a component. The default activity launched by the application is designated here.
uses-sdk	Related to the SDK version used by the application.

R.java

The R.java file is generated automatically when a project is created. It is a read-only file and cannot be modified. R.java is an index file defining all resources of the project. For example:

```
/* AUTO-GENERATED FILE.  DO NOT MODIFY.
     ... ...
 */
package com.example.helloandroid;
public final class R {
    public static final class attr {
    }
```

```java
public static final class dimen {
    public static final int padding_large=0x7f040002;
    public static final int padding_medium=0x7f040001;
    public static final int padding_small=0x7f040000;
}
public static final class drawable {
    public static final int ic_action_search=0x7f020000;
    public static final int ic_launcher=0x7f020001;
}
public static final class id {
    public static final int menu_settings=0x7f080000;
}
public static final class layout {
    public static final int activity_my_main=0x7f030000;
}
public static final class menu {
    public static final int activity_my_main=0x7f070000;
}
public static final class string {
    public static final int app_name=0x7f050000;
    public static final int hello_world=0x7f050001;
    public static final int menu_settings=0x7f050002;
    public static final int title_activity_my_main=0x7f050003;
}
public static final class style {
    public static final int AppTheme=0x7f060000;
}
}
```

You can see that many constants are defined in this code. The names of these constants are the same as the file names in the res folder, which proves that the R.java file stores the index of all resources of the project. With this file, it is more convenient to use resources in applications and identify the resources required. Because this file does not allow manual editing, you only need to refresh the project when adding new resources to it. The R.java file automatically generates the index of all resources.

Definition File of Constants

The values subdirectory of the project contains a definition file for the strings, colors, and array constants; the string constant definitions are in the strings.xml file. These constants are used by other files in the Android project.

Eclipse provides two graphic view tabs, Resources and strings.xml, for the strings.xml file. The Resources tab provides a structured view of the name-value, and the strings.xml tab directly displays the contents of a text file format. The strings.xml file of the HelloAndroid example is shown in Figure 1-6.

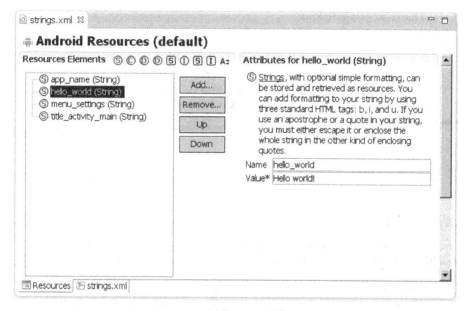

(a) Resource View

(b) XML view

Figure 1-6. *IDE graphic view of the* `strings.xml` *file of HelloAndroid*

The file content is as follows:

```
<resources>

    <string name="app_name">HelloAndroid</string>
    <string name="hello_world">Hello world!</string>
    <string name="menu_settings">Settings</string>
    <string name="title_activity_main">MainActivity</string>

</resources>
```

The code is very simple; it only defines four string constants (resources).

Layout Files

Layout files describe the size, location, and arrangement of each screen *widget* (combination of *window* and *gadget*). A layout file is the "face" of the application. Layout files are text files in XML format.

Widgets are visual UI elements, such as buttons and text boxes. They are equivalent to controls and containers in the Windows system terminology. Buttons, text boxes, scroll bars, and so forth are widgets. In the Android OS, widgets generally belong to the View class and its descendant classes and are stored in the android.widget package.

An application has a main layout file corresponding to the application's screen display at startup. For example, the layout file and the main interface of the HelloAndroid example are shown in Figure 1-7. When an application is created, Eclipse automatically generates a layout file for the application's main screen display. The file is located in the project folder's res\layout directory. The file name in the generated application projects is specified in the next section: in this case, the source code file name corresponds to the [Layout Name] key, so the file is named activity_main.xml.

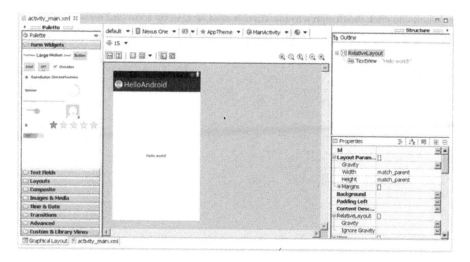

(a) The main graphic layout file in Eclipse

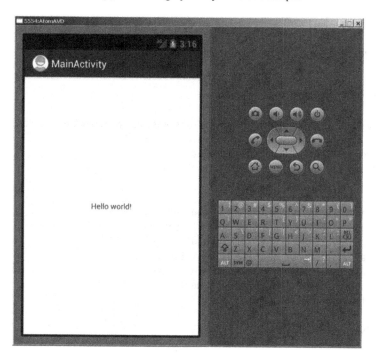

(b) The user interface

Figure 1-7. *The main graphic layout and user interface*

When you click the design window (in this case, `activity_main.xml`), you can see the corresponding contents of the XML-formatted text file, as shown in Figure 1-8.

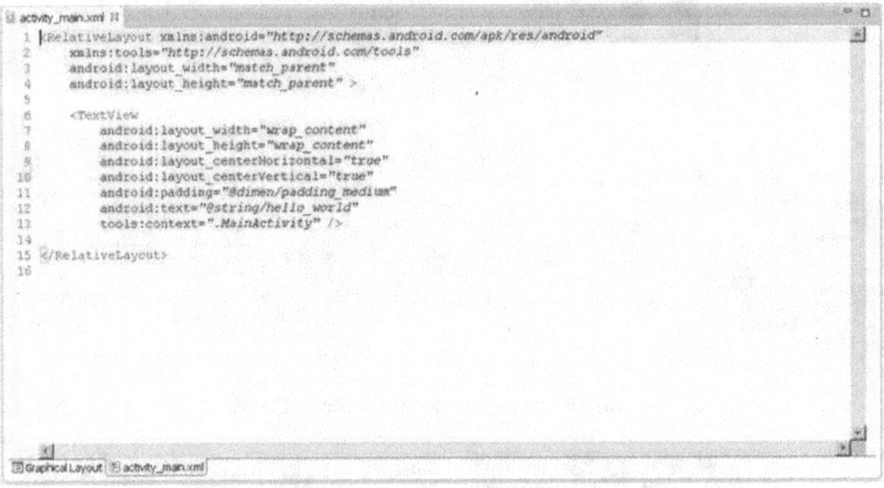

Figure 1-8. *The main layout file of the HelloAndroid example*

The contents of the file are as follows:

```xml
<RelativeLayout xmlns:android="http://schemas.android.com/apk/res/android"
    xmlns:tools="http://schemas.android.com/tools"
    android:layout_width="match_parent"
    android:layout_height="match_parent" >

    <TextView
        android:layout_width="wrap_content"
        android:layout_height="wrap_content"
        android:layout_centerHorizontal="true"
        android:layout_centerVertical="true"
        android:padding="@dimen/padding_medium"
        android:text="@string/hello_world"
        tools:context=".MainActivity" />

</RelativeLayout>
```

In this code, there are several layout parameters:

- `<RelativeLayout>`: The layout configuration for the relative position.

- `android:layout_width`: Customizes the screen width of the current view; `match_parent` represents the parent container (in this case, the activity) match; `fill_parent` fills the entire screen; `wrap_content`, expressed as text fields, changes depending on the width or height of this view.

- `android:layout_height`: Customizes the screen height occupied by the current view.

Two other common parameters, not shown in this layout file, are as follows:

- `android:orientation`: Here means the layout is arranged horizontally.

- `android:layout_weight`: Give a value for the importance assigned to multiple views of a linear layout. All views are given a `layout_weight` value; the default is zero.

Although the layout file is an XML file, you do not have to understand its format or directly edit it, because the Android Development Tools and Eclipse provide a visual design interface. You simply drag and drop widgets and set the corresponding properties in Eclipse, and your actions are automatically recorded in the layout file. You can see how this works when you walk though the application development example in following sections.

Source Code File

When a project is built, Eclipse generates a default `.java` source code file that contains the application basic runtime code for the project. It is located in the project folder under the `src\com\example\XXX` directory (where XXX is the project name). The file name of the generated application projects in this case is the source code file name that corresponds to the [Activity Name] key, so the file is named `MainActivity.java`.

The content of `MainActivity.java` is as follows:

```
package com.example.flashlight;

import android.os.Bundle;
import android.app.Activity;
import android.view.Menu;
import android.view.MenuItem;
import android.support.v4.app.NavUtils;
```

```
public class MyMainActivity extends Activity {
    @Override
    public void onCreate(Bundle savedInstanceState) {
        super.onCreate(savedInstanceState);
        setContentView(R.layout.activity_my_main);
    }
    @Override
    public boolean onCreateOptionsMenu(Menu menu) {
        getMenuInflater().inflate(R.menu.activity_my_main, menu);
        return true;
    }
}
```

Component Structure of Applications

The Android application framework provides APIs for developers. Because the application is built in Java, the first level of the program contains the UI needs of the various controls. For example, views (View components) contain lists, grids, text boxes, buttons, and even an embedded web browser.

An Android application usually consists of five components:

- Activity

- Intent receiver

- Service

- Content provider

- Intent and intent filters

The following sections discuss each components a bit more.

Activity

Applications with visual UIs are implemented using activities. When a user selects an application from the main screen or an application launcher, it starts an action or an activity. Each activity program typically takes the form of a separate interface (screen). Each activity is a separate class that extends and implements the activity's base class. This class is shown as the UI, consisting of View components responding to events.

Most programs have multiple activities (in other words, an Android application is composed of one or more activities). Switching to another interface loads a new activity. In some cases, a previous activity may give a return value. For example, an activity that lets the user select a photo returns the photo to the caller.

When a user opens a new interface, the old interface is suspended and placed in the history stack (interface-switching history stack). The user can go back to an activity that has been opened in the history stack interface. A stack that has no historical value can be removed from the history stack interface. Android retains all generated interfaces in the history stack for running the application, from the first interface to the last one.

An activity is a container, which itself is not displayed in the UI. You can roughly imagine an activity as a window in the Windows OS, but the view window is not only for displaying but also for completing a task.

Intent and Intent Filters

Android achieves interface switching through a special class called intent. An intent describes what the program does. The two most important parts of the data structure are the action and the data processed in accordance with established rules (data). Typical operations are MAIN (activity entrance), VIEW, PICK, and EDIT. Data to be used in the operation is presented using a Universal Resource Identifier (URI). For example, to view a person's contact information, you need to create an intent using the VIEW operation, and the data is a pointer to the person's URI.

A class associated with an intent is called an IntentFilter. An intent encapsulates a request as an object; IntentFilter then describes what intentions an activity (or, say, an intent receiver, explained in a moment) can process. In the previous example, the activity that shows a person's contact information uses an IntentFilter, and it knows how to handle the data VIEW operation applied to this person. The activity in the AndroidManifest.xml file using IntentFilter is usually accomplished by parsing the intent activity switch. First, it uses the startActivity (myIntent) function to start the new activity, next it systematically checks the IntentFilter of all installed programs, and then it finds the activity that is the best match with the myIntent corresponding to IntentFilter. This new activity receives the message from intent and then starts. The intent-resolution process occurs in real time in the startActivity called. This process has two advantages:

- The activity emits only one intent request and can reuse the function of other components.

- The activity can always be replaced by an equivalent new activity of the IntentFilter.

Service

A *service* is a resident system program that has no UI. You should use a service for any application that needs to run continuously, such as a network monitor or checking for application updates.

The two ways of using a service are *start-stop mode* and *bind-unbind mode*. The process flow chart and functions are shown in Table 1-3.

Table 1-3. *The Usage Model of a Service*

Mode	Start	End	Visit	Notes
Start/ stop	Context. startService()	Context. stopService()		Even if the process of the startService call is ended, the service is still there until the process calls stopService() or the service causes its own demise (stopSelf() is called).
Bind/ unbind	Context. bindService()	Context. unbindService()	Context. Service Connection()	When calling bindService(), the process is dead; then the service it binds to must be ended.

When two modes are in mixed use—for example, one mode calls startService() and other modes call bindService()—then only when both the stopService call and the unbindService call occur will the service be terminated.

A service process has its own life cycle, and Android tries to keep a service process that has been started or bound. The service process is described as follows:

- If the service is the implementation process of the method onCreate(), onStart, or onDestroy(), then the main process becomes a foreground process to ensure that this code is not stopped.

- If the service has started, the value of its importance is lower than that of the visible process but above all invisible processes. Because only a few processes are visible to the user, as long as the memory is not particularly low, the service does not stop.

- If multiple clients have bound to the service, as long as any one of the clients is visible to the user, that service is visible.

Broadcast Intent Receiver

When you want to execute some code associated with external events, such as have a task performed in the middle of the night or respond to a phone ringing, use IntentReceiver. Intent receivers have no UI and use NotificationManager to inform users that their event has happened. An intent receiver is declared in the AndroidManifest.xml file but can also be declared using Context.registerReceiver(). The program does not have to run continuously to wait for IntentReceiver to be called. When an intent receiver is triggered, the system starts your program. Programs can also use `Context.broadcastIntent()` to send their intent broadcast to other programs.

Android applications can be used to handle a data element or to respond to an event (such as receiving text messages). Android applications are deployed to the device together with an `AndroidManifest.xml` file. `AndroidManifest.xml` contains the necessary configuration information, so the application is properly installed on the device. `AndroidManifest.xml` also includes the necessary class names and the types of events that can be handled by the application, as well as the necessary permissions to run the application. For example, if an application needs to access the network—to, say, download a file—the manifest file must be explicitly listed in the license. Many applications may enable this particular license. This declarative security can help reduce the possibility of damage to equipment from malicious applications.

Content Provider

You can think of content providers as database servers. A content provider's task is to manage persistent data access, such as a SQLite database. If the application is very simple, you might not need to create a content-provider application. If you want to build a larger application or need to build applications to provide data for multiple activities or applications, you can use the content provider for data access.

If you want other programs to use their own programs' data, a content provider is very useful. The content-provider class implements a series of standard methods that allows other programs to store and read data that can be processed by the content provider.

Android Emulator

Android does not use the ordinary Java virtual machine (JVM); it uses the Dalvik virtual machine (DVM) instead. The DVM and JVM are fundamentally different. The DVM takes up less memory, is specifically optimized for mobile devices, and is more suitable for mobile phones used in embedded environments. Other differences are as follows:

- The general JVM is based on the stack-based virtual machine, but the DVM is a register-based virtual machine. The latter is better because applications can achieve maximum optimization based on the hardware, which is more in line with the characteristics of mobile devices.

- The DVM can run multiple virtual machine instances simultaneously in limited memory, so that each DVM application executes as a separate Linux process. In the general JVM, all applications run in a shared JVM, and therefore individual applications are not running as separate processes. With each application running as a separate process, the DVM can be prevented from closing all programs in the event of the collapse of the virtual machine.

- The DVM provides a less restrictive license platform than the general JVM. The DVM and JVM support different generic code. The DVM does not run standard Java bytecode, but rather Dalvik executable format (.dex). Java code compilation of Android applications actually consists of two processes. The first step is to compile the Java source code into normal JVM executable code, which uses the file-name suffix .class. The second step is to compile the bytecode into Dalvik execution code, which uses the file-name suffix .dex. The first step compiles the source code files under the src subdirectory in the project directory into .class files in the bin\class directory; and the second step moves the files from the bin\class subdirectory to classes.dex files in the bin directory. The compilation process is integrated into the Eclipse build process; however, you can also use the command line to compile manually.

Introducing Android Runtime (ART)

ART is an Android runtime that first became available in Google Android KitKat (4.4) as a preview feature. It is also called Dalvik version 2 and is under active development in the Android Open Source Project (AOSP). All smartphones and tablets with Android KitKat keep Dalvik as the default runtime. This is because some OEMs still do not support ART in Android implementations, and most third-party applications are still built based on Dalvik and have not yet added support for the new ART.

As described by Google on the Android developer site, most existing apps should work when running with ART. However, some techniques that work on Dalvik do not work on ART. The differences between Dalvik and ART are shown in Table 1-4.

Table 1-4. *Dalvik vs. ART Summary*

	Dalvik	ART
Application	APK package with DEX class file	Same as Dalvik
Compile Type	Dynamic compilation (JIT)	Ahead-of-time compilation (AOT)
Functionality	Stable and went through extensive QA	Basic functionality and stability
Installation Time	Faster	Slower due to compilation
App Launch Time	Mostly slower due to JIT compilation and interpretation	Mostly faster due to AOT compilation
Storage Footprint	Smaller	Larger, with precompiled binary
Memory Footprint	Larger due to JIT code cache	Smaller

ART offers some new features to help with application development, performance optimization, and debugging, such as support for the sampling profiler and debugging features like monitoring and garbage collection. Transitioning from Dalvik to ART is likely to take some time, and Dalvik and ART will both be provided in Android to allow smartphone and tablet users to select and switch. However, future 64-bit Android will be based on ART.

Summary

This chapter introduced the general GUI design method for desktop systems and then showed how designing the UI and UX for embedded systems is different. You should now understand the general methods and principles of GUI design for Android applications and be ready to learn about the Android-specific GUI. The next chapter describes the state transition of activities, the Context class, intent, and the relationship between applications and activities.

CHAPTER 2

■ ■ ■

GUI Design for Android Apps, Part 2: The Android-Specific GUI

This chapter describes the state transitions of activities and discusses the Context class, intent, and the relationship between applications and activities.

State Transitions of Activities

As mentioned in Chapter 1, the activity is the most important component. Activities have their own state and transition rules, and they are the basis of what you need to understand to write Android applications.

Activity States

When activities are created or destroyed, they enter or exit the activity stack. And as they do, they transition among four possible states:

> *Active*: An activity in the active state is visible when it is on the top of the stack. Typically, it is the foreground activity that is responding to user input. Android will ensure that it executes at all costs. If required, Android will destroy stack activities further down to ensure required resources for the active activity. When another activity becomes active, this activity is paused.

Paused: In some cases, an activity is visible but does not have focus. At this moment, it is suspended. When the active activity is fully transparent or is the non-full screen activity, the activity below reaches this state. Paused activities are considered active but do not accept user input events. In extreme cases, Android will kill a paused activity to restore resources to the active activity. When an activity is completely invisible, it becomes stopped.

Stopped: When an activity is not visible, it is stopped. This activity remains in memory to save all state and member information. But when the system needs memory, this activity is "taken out and shot." When an activity stops, it is very important to save the data and the current UI state. Once the activity exits or is closed, it becomes inactive.

Inactive: When an activity is killed, it becomes inactive. Inactive activities are removed from the activity stack. When you need to use or display the activity, it needs to be started again.

The activity state transition diagram is shown in Figure 2-1.

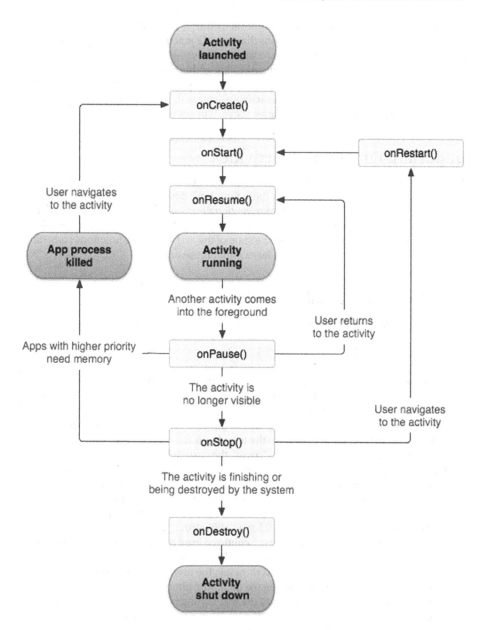

Figure 2-1. *Android activity state transition diagram*

State change is not artificial and is controlled entirely by the Android memory manager. Android first closes applications that contain inactive activities, followed by those with stopped activities. In extreme cases, it removes paused activities.

To ensure a flawless user experience, transition of these states is invisible to users. When an activity returns to active status from the paused, stopped, or inactive state, the UI must be nondiscriminatory. So, when an activity is stopped, it is very important to save the UI state and data. Once an activity becomes active, it needs to recover the saved values.

Important Functions of Activities

The activity state transition triggers the function of the corresponding activity class (that is, the Java method). Android calls these functions; developers do not have to explicitly call them. They are called *state-transition functions*. You can override the state-transition functions so they can complete their work at the specified time. There are also some functions that are used to control the state of the activity. These functions constitute the basis of activity programming. Let's learn about those functions.

onCreate State-Transition Function

The onCreate function prototype is as follows:

```
void  onCreate(Bundle savedInstanceState);
```

This function is run when the activity is first loaded. When you start a new program, its main activity's onCreate event is executed. If the activity is destroyed (OnDestroy, explained later) and then reloaded into the task, its onCreate event participants are re-executed.

An activity is likely to be forced to switch to the background. (An activity switched to the background is no longer visible to the user, but it still exists in the middle of a task, such as when a new activity is started to "cover" the current activity; or the user presses the Home button to return to the home screen; or other events occur in the new activity on top of the current activity, such as an incoming caller interface.) If the user does not view the activity again after a period of time, the activity may be automatically destroyed by the system along with the task and process. If you check the activity again, the onCreate event initialization activity will have to be rerun.

And sometimes you may want users to continue from the last open operating state of the activity, rather than starting from scratch. For example, when the user receives a sudden incoming call while editing a text message, the user may have to do other things immediately after the call, such as saving the incoming phone number to a contact. If the user does not immediately return to the text-editing interface, the text-editing interface is destroyed. As a result, when the user returns to the SMS program, that user may want to continue from the last edit. In this case, you can override the activity's void onSaveInstanceState (Bundle outState) events by writing the data you want to be saved before the destruction of the state of activity or information through outState, so that when the activity executes the onCreate event again, it transmits information previously saved through the savedInstanceState. At this point, you can selectively use the information to initialize the activity, instead of starting it from scratch.

onStart State-Transition Function

The onStart function prototype is as follows:

```
void onStart();
```

The onStart function executes after the onCreate event or when the current activity is switched to the background. When the user switches back to this activity by selecting it from switch panel, if it has not been destroyed, and only the onStop event has been performed, the activity will skip onCreate event activities and directly execute onStart events.

onResume State-Transition Function

The onResume function prototype is as follows:

```
void onResume()
```

The onResume function is executed after the OnStart event or after the current activity is switched to the background. When the user views this activity again, if it has not been destroyed, and if onStop events have not been performed (activities continue to exist in the task), the activity will skip onCreate and onStart event activities and directly execute onResume events.

onPause State-Transition Function

The onPause function prototype is as follows:

```
void onPause()
```

The onPause function is executed when the current activity is switched to the background.

onStop State-Transition Function

The onStop function prototype is as follows:

```
void onStop()
```

The onStop function is executed after the onPause event. If the user does not view the activity again for some time, the onStop event of the activity is executed. The onStop events are also executed if the user presses the Back key, and the activity is removed from the current task list.

onRestart State-Transition Function

The onRestart function prototype is as follows:

```
void onRestart()
```

After the onStop event is executed, if the activity and the process it resides in have not been systematically destroyed, or if the user views the activity again, the onRestart event(s) of the activity are executed. The onRestart event skips the onCreate event activities and directly executes the onStart events.

onDestroy State-Transition Function

The onDestroy function prototype is as follows:

```
void onDestroy()
```

After an onStop event of the activity, if the user does not view the activity again, it is destroyed.

The finish Function

The finish function prototype is as follows:

```
void finish()
```

The finish function closes the activity and removes it from the stack, which leads to a call to the onDestroy() state-transition function. One way to resolve this is for the user to navigate to the previous activity using the Back button.

In addition to the activity switch, the finish function triggers the activity's state-transition function, and the startActivity and startActivityForResult methods of the context class (described in the next sections) also activate it. Functions such as Context.startActivity also cause the construction of activity objects (that is, create new ones).

Typical causes of the triggers and corresponding functions are listed in Table 2-1.

Table 2-1. *Triggers and Their Functions*

Typical Trigger Cause	Corresponding Method of Activity Executed	Explanations

`Context.`
`startActivity[ForResult]()`
Note: As long as the activity is displayed and viewable on the screen, this method will be called.
	`new Activity()`
	
	`onCreate()`
		Completes the constructor function, Saves the `activity` object to the application object, and initializes the various controls (such as `View`).

	`onStart()`	Similar to `View.onDraw()`.
`Activity.finish()`	`onDestroy()`	Completes the constructor function, such as removing the `activity` object from the application.

Functions such as `Context.startActivity` in Table 2-1 trigger three actions: constructing new `Activity` objects, `onCreate`, and `onStart`. When an activity that is moved from off screen places to the top of the screen display (that is, displayed in front of the user), it generally only includes functions being called by `onStart`.

The Context Class

The `Context` class is an important Android concept to know. The class is inherited from the `Object` function, whose inheritance is as follows:

```
java.lang.Object
 ↳ android.content.Context
```

The literal meaning of *context* is the text in the adjacent area, which is located in the `android.content.Context` of the framework package. The `Context` class is a `LONG` type, similar to the `Handle` handler in Win32. `Context` provides the global information interface about the application environment. It is an abstract class, and its execution is provided by the Android system. It allows access to resources and characterized types of applications. At the same time, it can start application-level operations, such as starting activities and broadcasting and receiving intents.

Many methods require the caller to be identified through a context instance. For example, the first parameter of `Toast` is `Context`; and usually you use `this` to replace the activity, which indicates that the caller's instance is an activity. But other methods, such as a button's `onClick (View view)`, cause errors if you use `this`. In this case, you may use

ActivityName.this to solve the problem, because the class implements the context of several major Android-specific models like activities, services, and broadcast receivers.

If the parameter—especially the constructor parameter of the class (such as Dialog)—is the Context type, the actual parameters are typically activity objects, generally [this]. For example, the Dialog constructor prototype is

```
Dialog.Dialog(Context context)
```

Here's an example:

```
public class MyActivity extends Activity{
    Dialog d = new Dialog(this);
```

Context is the ancestor of most classes of Android, such as broadcasting, intents, and so on, and it provides the interface of the global information application environment. Table 2-2 lists the important subclasses of Context. You can find a detailed description in the help documentation for the Android Context class.

Table 2-2. *Important Subclasses of* Context

Subclass	Explanation
Activity	User-friendly interface class
Application	Base class that provides global application state maintenance
IntentService	Base class used to handle asynchronous requests for the service (expressed in an Intent way)
Service	A component of the application that represents either a time-consuming operation that has no interaction with the user or a task that provides functionality for other application tasks

Classes are called *offspring classes* because they are direct or indirect subclasses of Context and have an inheritance relationship like activities:

```
java.lang.Object
  ↳ android.content.Context
    ↳ android.content.ContextWrapper
      ↳ android.view.ContextThemeWrapper
        ↳ android.app.Activity
```

Context can be used for many operations in Android, but it main function is to load and access resources. There are two commonly used contexts: the application context and the activity context. The activity context is usually passed between a variety of classes and methods, similar to the code of onCreate for an activity, as follows:

```
protected void onCreate(Bundle state) {
    super.onCreate(state);
    TextView label = new TextView(this); // Pass context to view control
    setContentView(label);
}
```

When the activity context is passed to the view, it means that view has a reference pointed to an activity and references resources taken by the activity: view hierarchy, resource, and so on.

You can also use the application context, which always accompanies the application's life but has nothing to do with the activity life cycle. The application context can be acquired with the Context.getApplicationContext or Activity.getApplication method.

Java usually uses a static variable (singleton and the like) to synchronize states between activities (between classes inside a program). Android's more reliable approach is to use the application context to associate these states.

Each activity has a context, which contains the runtime state. Similarly, an application has a context that Android uses to ensure that it is the only instance of that context.

If you need to make a custom application context, first you must define a custom class that inherits from android.app.Application; then describe the class in the application's AndroidManifest.xml file. Android automatically creates an instance of this class. By using the Context.getApplicationContext() method, you can get the application context inside each activity. The following example code gets the application context in the activity:

```
class MyApp extends Application {
// MyApp is a custom class inherited from android.app.Application
    public String aCertainFunc () {
        ......
    }
}

class Blah extends Activity {
    public void onCreate(Bundle b){
        ... ...
        MyApp appState = ((MyApp)getApplicationContext());
// Get Application Context
        appState.aCertainFunc();
//Use properties and methods of the application
        ... ...
    }
}
```

You can get global information about the application environment using the get function of Context. The main functions are shown in Table 2-3 and are either ContextWrapper or direct context methods.

Table 2-3. *Commonly Used Methods for Obtaining Context*

Function Prototype	Function
abstract Context ContextWrapper. getApplicationContext ()	Returns the current process corresponding to the global context of a single application.
abstract ApplicationInfo ContextWrapper.getApplicationInfo ()	Returns the context package corresponding to the information of the entire application.
abstract ContentResolver ContextWrapper.getContentResolver ()	Returns the content-resolver instance of the corresponding application package.
abstract PackageManager ContextWrapper.getPackageManager ()	Returns the package-manager instance for finding all package information.
abstract String ContextWrapper. getPackageName ()	Returns the current package name.
abstract Resources ContextWrapper. getResources ()	Returns the resource instance of the (user) application package.
abstract SharedPreferences ContextWrapper.getSharedPreferences (String name, int mode)	Finds and holds the contents of the preference file whose name is specified by the parameter name. Returns the value of the shared preferences (SharedPreferences) that you can find and modify. When using a proper name, only one instance of SharedPreferences is returned to the caller, which means once the changes are complete, the results are shared with each other.
public final String Context. getString (int resId)	Returns a localized string from the application package's default string table.
abstract Object ContextWrapper. getSystemService (String name)	Returns processing system-level services according to the name specified by the variable name. The returned object classes vary based on the name of the request.

Introduction to Intent

Intent can be used as a message-passing mechanism to allow you to declare intent to take an action, usually with specific data. You can use intent to implement interaction between components of any application on Android devices. Intent turns a group of independent components into systems with one-to-one interactions.

It can also be used to broadcast messages. Any application can register a broadcast receiver to listen and respond to these intent broadcasts. Intent can be used to create internal, system, or third-party event-driven applications.

Intent is responsible for the description of an operation and the action data of the application. Android is responsible for finding the corresponding component described under the sub-intent, passing intent to the component being called, and completing the component calls. Intent plays the decoupling role between the caller and the one who is called.

Intent is a mechanism of runtime binding; it can connect two different components in the process of running the program. Through intent, the program can request or express willingness to Android; Android selects the appropriate components to handle the request based on the contents of the intent. For example, suppose an activity wants to open a web browser to view the content of a page; this activity only needs to issue a WEB_SEARCH_ACTION request to Android. Based on the content request, Android will check the intent filter declared in the component registration statement and find an activity for a web browser.

When an intent is issued, Android finds one or more exact matches for the activity, service, or broadcastReceiver as a response. Therefore, different types of intent messages do not overlap and are not simultaneously sent to an activity or service, because startActivity() messages can be sent only to an activity and startService() intents can only be sent to a service.

The Main Roles of Intent

The main roles of intent are as follows.

Triggering a New Activity or Letting an Existing Activity Implement the New Operation

In Android, intent directly interacts with the activity. The most common use of intent is to bind application components. Intent is used to start, stop, and transfer application activities. In other words, intent can activate a new activity or make an existing activity perform a new operation. This can be accomplished by calling the Context.startActivity() or Context.startActivityForResult() method.

To open a different interface (corresponding to an activity) in an application, you call the Context.startActivity() function to pass an intent. Intent can either explicitly specify a specific class to open or include an action required to achieve the goals. In the latter case, the runtime will choose which activity to open, using a well-known process of intent resolution in which the Context.startActivity() finds and starts a single activity that best matches the intent.

Triggering a New Service or Sending New Requests to Existing Services

Opening a service or sending a request to an existing service is also completed by the intent class.

Trigger BroadcastReceiver

You can send `BroadcastIntent` using three different methods: `Context.sendBroadcast()`, `Context.sendOrderedBroadcast()`, and `Context.sendStickyBroadcast()`.

Intent Resolution

The intent transfer process has two ways to match target consumers (such as another activity, `IntentReceiver`, or service) with the respondents of the intent.

The first is *explicit matching*, also known as *direct intent*. When constructing an `intent` object, you must specify the recipient as one of the intent's component properties (by calling `setComponent (ComponentName)` or `setClass (Context, Class)`). By specifying a component class, the application notification starts the corresponding components. This method is similar to an ordinary function call but varies in the reuse of the granularity.

The second is *implicit matching*, also known as *indirect intent*. The sender of the intent does not know or care who the recipient is when constructing an `intent` object. The attribute is not specified in the component intent. This intent needs to contain sufficient information so that the system can determine which components to use out of all those available to meet this intent. This method differs significantly from function calls and helps to reduce coupling between the sender and receiver. Implicit matching resolves to a single activity. If there are multiple activities that can implement a given action based on particular data, Android selects the best one to start.

For direct intent, Android does not need to do parsing because the target component is very clear. However, Android needs to resolve indirect intent. Through analysis, it maps the indirect intent to the activity, `IntentReceiver`, or service that processes the intent.

The mechanism of intent resolution mainly consists of the following:

- Looking for all `<intent-filter>`s and the intent defined by those filters, which are registered in `AndroidManifest.xml`

- Finding and handling the component of the intent through `PackageManager` (`PackageManager` can get information about the application package installed on the current device)

Intent filters are very important. A non-declared `<intent-filter>` component can only respond to explicit intent requests that the component name matches, but it cannot respond to implicit intent requests. A declared `<intent-filter>` component can respond to either explicit intent or implicit intent requests. When resolving implicit intent requests, Android uses three attributes of the intent—action, type, and category—to make the resolution. The specific resolution methods are described next.

Action Test

A `<intent-filter>` element should contain at least one `<action>`, or no intent requests can be matched to the `<intent-filter>`. If the action requested by an intent has at least one match of an `<action>` in `<intent-filter>`, then the intent passed the action test of this `<intent-filter>`.

If there is no description of a specific action type in the intent request or `<intent-filter>`, then one of the two following tests applies:

- If `<intent-filter>` does not contain any action type, regardless of what the intent requests are, there is no match to this `<intent-filter>`.

- If the intent request has no set action type, as long as the `<intent-filter>` contains an action type, this intent request will successfully pass the action test of `<intent-filter>`.

Category Test

For an intent to pass the category test, every category in the Intent must match a category in the filter. When every category of intent requests have exact matches with the `<category>` of one `<intent-filter>` of the components the intent request pass the test. The excess `<category>` declaration of `<intent-filter>` does not cause the match failure. Any `<intent-filter>` that does not specify a category test only matches intent requests that the configuration is not set for.

Data Test

The `<data>` element specifies a data URI and data type of the intent request that you want to receive. A URI is divided into three parts that match: scheme, authority, and path. The URI data type and scheme of the Internet request set by `setData()` must be the same as specified in `<intent-filter>`. If `<intent-filter>` also specifies authority or path, they have to match to pass the test.

This decision process can be expressed as follows:

- If the intent specifies the action, then the action list of the `<intent-filter>` of the target component must contain this action. Otherwise, it is not considered matched.

- If the intent does not provide a type, the system gets the data types from the data. And for some action methods, the target component's data-type list must contain the data type of the intent. Otherwise it cannot be matched.

- If the data for the intent is not the URI of the content, and the category and intent also do not specify its type, the matching is based on the data scheme of the intent (for instance, `http:` or `mailto:`), and the intent's scheme must appear in the scheme list of the target component.

- If the intent specifies one or more categories, these categories must all appear in the category list of the component. For instance, if the intent contains two categories, LAUNCHER_ CATEGORY and ALTERNATIVE_CATEGORY, the target component obtained by the parsing must contain at least these two categories.

The Relationship between Applications and Activities

Beginners tend to get confused between applications and activities—in particular, the main activities (those that occur when the application starts). In fact, they are two completely different objects. The behaviors, attributes, and so forth are not the same. Following is a list of differences between applications and activities:

- No matter how many times an application starts, as long as it is not shut down, its value (that is, the object) is constant. It has only one instance.

- No matter where an application starts, as long as it is not closed, its value (that is, the object) is constant. It has only one instance.

- When an activity is not finished, its value (that is, the object) is constant. Each time onStart() is called, the activity displays on the screen front.

- The objects that startActivity starts are different each time. You can say that startActivity actually contains new objects.

  - Although you cannot get a new activity object after startActivity, the Android framework can send parameter values (similar to the actual parameter of the function call) when startActivity starts its corresponding activity objects.

  - Even more surprising is that Android can have an activity coexist in multiple objects. When an activity is closed, Android returns the results to the main activity started through startActivity. As a result, it automatically calls the onActivityResult() method that starts its activity object, and random distribution can be avoided.

- An application can have multiple objects of an activity.

The Basic Android Application Interface

In this section, you use an example to learn about Android development using the Android SDK integrated in the Eclipse IDE. You create an application named GuiExam using the Android SDK and learn about the Android interface design by following the steps of the process.

GuiExam Application Code Analysis

This section provides analysis of the GuiExam sample application. First, let's create the GuiExam application using the Android SDK in Eclipse. For the application name, type GuiExam. For the Build SDK, choose API 19, which includes the x86 instructions. As shown in Figure 2-2, select the system default configurations for all other entries.

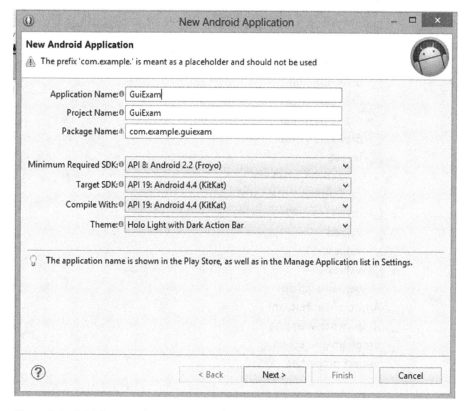

Figure 2-2. *Initial setup when generating the GuiExam project*

The file structure of the project is shown in Figure 2-3, and the user interface is shown in Figure 2-4.

Figure 2-3. *File structure of the GuiExam application*

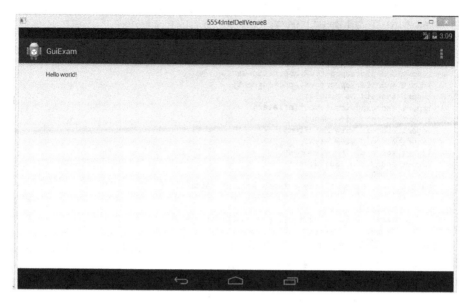

Figure 2-4. *The application interface of GuiExam*

The source code of the application's only Java file (`MainActivity.java`) is shown in Figure 2-5:

```
📄 MainActivity.java ⊠   📄 fragment_main.xml
 1  package com.example.guiexam;
 2
 3⊖ import android.support.v7.app.ActionBarActivity;
 4  import android.support.v7.app.ActionBar;
 5  import android.support.v4.app.Fragment;
 6  import android.os.Bundle;
 7  import android.view.LayoutInflater;
 8  import android.view.Menu;
 9  import android.view.MenuItem;
10  import android.view.View;
11  import android.view.ViewGroup;
12  import android.os.Build;
13
14  public class MainActivity extends ActionBarActivity {
15
16⊖     @Override
17      protected void onCreate(Bundle savedInstanceState) {
18          super.onCreate(savedInstanceState);
19          setContentView(R.layout.activity_main);
20
21          if (savedInstanceState == null) {
22              getSupportFragmentManager().beginTransaction()
23                      .add(R.id.container, new PlaceholderFragment())
24                      .commit();
25          }
26      }
27
28
29⊖     @Override
30      public boolean onCreateOptionsMenu(Menu menu) {
31
32          // Inflate the menu; this adds items to the action bar if it is present.
33          getMenuInflater().inflate(R.menu.main, menu);
34          return true;
35      }
36
```

Figure 2-5. *The typical source codes in Java file MainActivity.java*

You know the MainActivity.OnCreate() function is called when the event is created. The source code of the function is very simple. The superclass function is called in line 12, and the setContentView function is called in line 13. This function sets the UI display of the activity. In the Android project, most of the UI is realized by the view and view subclasses. View represents a region that can handle the event and can also render this region.

The code in line 13 indicates that the view is R.layout.activity_main. The auto-generated R.Java file under the gen directory of the project includes code such as this (excerpted):

```
Line #    Source Code
......
8 package com.example.guiexam;
9
```

```
10 public final class R {
      ......
26     public static final class layout {
27          public static final int activity_main=0x7f030000;
28     }
29     public static final class id {
30          public static final int menu_settings=0x7f080000;
31     }
32     public static final class string {
33          public static final int app_name=0x7f050000;
34          public static final int hello_world=0x7f050001;
35          public static final int menu_settings=0x7f050002;
36          public static final int title_activity_main=0x7f050003;
37     }
      ......
41     }
```

You can see that R.layout.activity_main is the resource ID of the main layout file activity_main.xml. This file reads as follows:

```
Line#     Source Code
1 <RelativeLayout xmlns:android="http://schemas.android.com/apk/res/android"
2     xmlns:tools="http://schemas.android.com/tools"
3     android:layout_width="match_parent"
4     android:layout_height="match_parent" >
5
6     <TextView
7          android:layout_width="wrap_content"
8          android:layout_height="wrap_content"
9          android:layout_centerHorizontal="true"
10          android:layout_centerVertical="true"
11          android:padding="@dimen/padding_medium"
12          android:text="@string/hello_world"
13          tools:context=".MainActivity" />14
15 </RelativeLayout>
```

The first line of this code indicates that the content is a RelativeLayout class. By checking the Android help documentation, you can see that the inheritance relationship of RelativeLayout is

```
java.lang.Object
   ↳ android.view.View
      ↳ android.view.ViewGroup
         ↳ android.widget.RelativeLayout
```

This class is indeed seen as a view class. This layout contains a TextView class, which is also the offspring class of the view. Line 12 indicates that its text property is @string/hello_world and its display text is the contents of the variable hello_world in strings.xml: "Hello world!"

As a superclass of the layout, ViewGroup is a special view that can contain other view objects or even ViewGroup itself. In other words, the ViewGroup object treats the objects of other views or ViewGroups as member variables (called *properties* in Java). The internal view objects contained in ViewGroup objects are called *widgets*. Because of the particularity of the ViewGroup, Android makes it possible for a variety of complex interfaces for applications to be automatically set.

Using Layouts as Interfaces

You can modify or design layouts as part of the application interface design. For example, you can modify the activity_main.xml file as follows:

1. Change TextView's Text property to "Type Here".

2. Pick a button widget from the Form Widgets column, and drop it into the activity_main screen. Set its Text property to "Click Me", as shown in Figure 2-6.

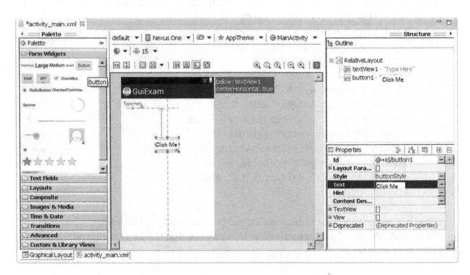

Figure 2-6. *Modifying the GuiExam layout to add a button*

3. Drag a plain text widget from the Text Fields section of the left column and drop it into the activity_main screen. Change the Width property under the layout parameters branch to fill_parent, and then drag plain text until it fills the entire layout, as shown in Figure 2-7.

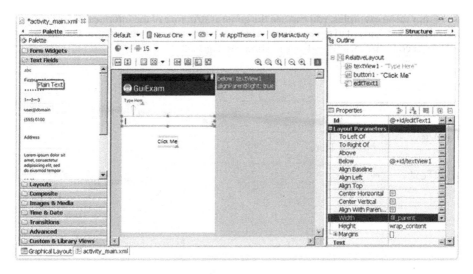

Figure 2-7. *Modifying the GuiExam layout to add a text-edit widget*

(a) Portrait Mode (b) Landscape Mode

Figure 2-8. *The user interface of GuiExam after the layout has been modified*

From these examples, you can see the general structure of the interface. The activity set through setContentView (layout file resource ID) is: the activity contains a layout, and the layout contains various widgets, as shown in Figure 2-9.

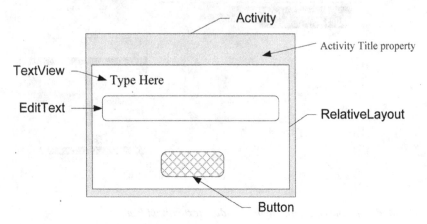

Figure 2-9. *Interface structure of the activity*

You may be wondering why Android introduced this layout concept. In fact, this is a developer-favored feature of Android, compared to the programming interface of Windows Microsoft Foundation Class (MFC). The layout isolates differences in screen size, orientation, and other details on the device, which makes the interface screen adaptive to a variety of devices. So, applications running on different device platforms can automatically adjust the size and position of the widget without the need for user intervention or code modification.

For example, the application you created can run on different Android phones, tablets, and television device platforms without your needing to change any code. The location and size of the widget are automatically adjusted. Even when you rotate a phone 90 degrees, the interface for portrait or landscape mode is automatically resized and maintained in its relative position. The layout also allows widgets to be arranged according to local national habits (most countries arrange them from left to right, but some countries arrange them from right to left). The details that need to be considered for the interface design are all completed by the layout. You can imagine what would happen if there were no layout classes—you would have to write code for each Android interface layout for each device. The complexity of this level of work is unthinkable.

Using the View Directly as an Interface

Earlier you saw an interface structure and code framework for activities. You also saw that most of the UI is implemented by the view and view subclasses. So, you can use the setContentView function to specify a view object, instead of a layout. The prototype of the setContentView function of the activity class includes the following.

This function sets a layout resource as the interface of the activity:

```
void setContentView(int layoutResID)
```

The first type of the function sets an explicit view as the interface of the activity:

```
void setContentView(View view)
```

The 2nd type f the function sets an explicit view as the interface of the activity, according to the specified format:

```
setContentView(View view, ViewGroup.LayoutParams params)
```

Here you work through an application example that uses the view directly as an activity interface, using the second function setContentView()You can modify the code of the MainActivity.java file as follows:

```
......
import android.widget.TextView;

public class MainActivity extends Activity {
    @Override
    public void onCreate(Bundle savedInstanceState) {
        super.onCreate(savedInstanceState);
        TextView tv = new TextView(this);      // Create a TextView Object
that belongs to current Activity
        tv.setText("Hello My friends!");        // Set Display text of TextView
        setContentView(tv);                     // Set View as the main display
of the Activity
}
```

The application interface is shown in Figure 2-10.

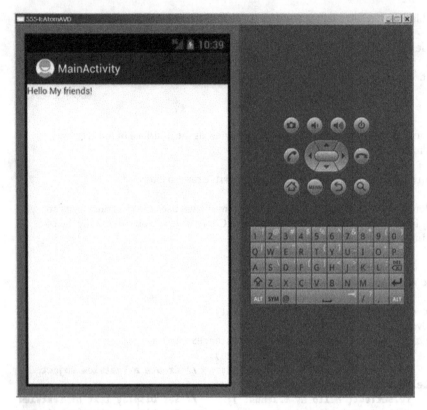

Figure 2-10. *GuiExam sets the view directly as the interface*

In this case you have TextView widgets, which are direct descendant classes of the view, as the application interface; they are set directly in the setContentView function. This way, the text displayed by the TextView becomes the output of the application interface. To use the TextView class, you use an import android.widget.TextView statement at the beginning of the file to import the package of the class.

Component ID

Now let's go back and look at the application layout shown in Figure 2-6. The ID attribute of the added text-edit widget in the layout is @ + id/editText1, and the button's ID property is @ + id/button1 (as shown in Figure 2-5). What does that mean?

Let's look at the R.java file (excerpted):

```
Line #    Source Code
   ......
8 package com.example.guiexam;
9
```

```
10 public final class R {
   ......
22    public static final class id {
23        public static final int button1=0x7f080001;
24        public static final int editText1=0x7f080002;
25        public static final int menu_settings=0x7f080003;
26        public static final int textView1=0x7f080000;
27    }
28    public static final class layout {
29        public static final int activity_main=0x7f030000;
30    }
   ......
43 }
```

Compared with the R.java file in the "GuiExam Application" section, you can see that lines 23 and 24 are new; they are the resource ID number of the newly added button and text-edit box. The type is int, which corresponds to the ID attribute values of these widgets. From the R.java file, you can find the ID of these widgets—the static constant R.id.button1 is the resource ID of the widgets (buttons) for which the ID attribute value is @ + id/button1, and the static constant R.id.editText1 is the resource ID of the widgets (text edit) for which the ID attribute value is @ + id/editText1. What's the reason for this? Let's see.

Android components (including widgets and activities) need to use a value of type int as a tag This value is the ID attribute value of the component tag. The ID attribute can only accept a value of resources type. That is, the value must start with @, ; for example, @ id/abc, @+id/xyz, and so on.

The @ symbol is used to prompt the parser for XML files to parse the name behind the @. For example, for @string/button1, the parser reads the button1 value of this variable from values/string.xml.

If the + symbol is used right after the @, it means that when you modify and save a layout file, the system will automatically generate the corresponding type int variables in R.java. The variable name is the value after the / symbol; for example, @+id/xyz generates int xyz = value in R.java, where the value is a hexadecimal number. If the same variable name xyz already exists in R.java, the system does not generate a new variable; instead, the component uses this existing variable.

In other words, if you use the @+id/name format and a variable named name exists in R.java, the component will use the value of the variable as an identifier. If the variable does not exist, the system adds a new variable, and the corresponding value for the variable is assigned (not repeated).

Because the component's ID attribute can be a resource ID, you can set any existing resource ID value: for example, @drawable/icon, @string/ok, or @+string/. Of course, you can also set a resource ID that already exists in the Android system, such as @id/android:list, in which the android: modifier in the ID indicates the package where the R class of the system is located (in the R.java file). You can enter android.R.id in the Java code-editing zone, which lists the corresponding resource ID. For example, you can set the ID property value this way.

For the reason just described, you generally set the ID attributes of Android components (including widgets, activities, and so on) to the @+id/XXX format. And you use R.id.XXX to represent the component's resource ID number in the program.

Buttons and Events

In the example in the section "Using Layouts as Interfaces," you created an application that includes Button, EditText, and other widgets, but nothing happens when the button is clicked. This is because you did not assign a response to the click event. This section first introduces Android events and the basics of the listener functions. You review and further explore more advanced knowledge about events in future chapters covering Android's multithreaded design.

In Android, each application maintains an event loop. When an application starts, it completes the appropriate initialization and then enters the event loop state, where it waits for a user action such as clicking the touch screen, pressing a key (a button), or some other input operation. User action triggers the program to generate a response to the *event*; the system generates and distributes the corresponding event class to handle it according to the event location, such as Activity or View. The callback methods are integrated into an interface called the *event listener*. You can achieve the specified event response by overriding the abstraction functions of the interface.

The scope of the event received by different classes is different for each class. For example, the Activity class can receive keypress events but not touch events, whereas the View class can receive both touch and keypress events. In addition, the event attribute details received by different classes also vary. For example, the touch event received by the View class consists of a number of touch points, coordinate values, and other information. It is subdivided into pressing down, bouncing, and moving events. But the Button class, which is a descendent of the View class, only detects a pressing action, and the event does not provide the coordinates of touch points or other information. In other words, Button processes the original event of the view and integrates all touch events into one event that records whether it is *clicked* or not.

Most of the incident-response interfaces of the View class use Listener as a suffix, so it is easy to remember their association with the event-listener interface. Table 2-4 shows examples of a number of classes and their incident-response functions.

Table 2-4. Examples of Classes and Their Incident-Response Functions

Class	Event	Listener Interface and Function
Button	Click	onClick() function of the onClickListener Interface
RadioGroup	Click	onCheckChange() function of the onCheckChangeListener Interface
View	Drop-down list	onTouch() function of the TouchListener interface
	Input focus changes	onFocusChange() function of the onFocusChangeListener interface
	Button	onKey() function of the onKeyListener interface

The process to respond to events is as follows. First, define the implementation class of your listener interface and override the abstract function. Second, call functions such as set ... Listener(). Then set the implementation class of the custom monitor interface to the event listener of the corresponding objects.

For example, you can modify the application source to execute an incident response. There are many coding styles to implement a Java interface. The next section discusses several ways in which the results of the code running these styles is the same.

Inner Class Listener

Modify the MainActivity.java code as follows (the bold text is added or modified):

```
Line #     Source Code
1 package com.example.guiexam;
2 import android.os.Bundle;
3 import android.app.Activity;
4 import android.view.Menu;
5 import android.view.MenuItem;
6 import android.support.v4.app.NavUtils;
7 import android.widget.TextView;

8 import android.widget.Button;              // Use Button class
9
10 import android.view.View;                  // Use View class
11 import android.view.View.OnClickListener;  // Use View.OnClickListener
   class
12 import android.util.Log;
13 // Use Log.d debugging function
   public class MainActivity extends Activity {
14     private int iClkTime = 1;
15
16 // Count of Button Click
17
   @Override
18     public void onCreate(Bundle savedInstanceState) {
19         super.onCreate(savedInstanceState);
20         setContentView(R.layout.activity_main);
21
22         Button btn = (Button) findViewById(R.id.button1);
23 // Obtain Button object based on the resource ID number
24         final String prefixPrompt ="This is No. ";
25 // Define and set the value of the variable passed
26         final String suffixPrompt ="time(s) that Button is clicked";
```

```
27 // Define and set the value of the variable passed
28         btn.setOnClickListener(new /*View.*/OnClickListener(){
29 // Set the event response class of Button's click
30
31            public void onClick(View v) {
32                Log.d("ProgTraceInfo",prefixPrompt + (iClkTime++) +
                   suffixPrompt);

         }
      });
   }

   @Override
   public boolean onCreateOptionsMenu(Menu menu) {
       getMenuInflater().inflate(R.menu.activity_main, menu);
       return true;
   }
}
```

On lines 18-22, you get the corresponding objects based on the resource ID of EditText and TextView, respectively. To use OnClickListener as an internal class, you add the final modifier in front of the variable. In lines 23 and 24, as the response code of the Button clicks, you first get the contents of EditText using EditText.getText(). Because the function returns a value of type Editable, you convert the type Editable to the type String via the CharSequence.toString() function (CharSequence is a superclass of Editable). Then you call the TextView.setText (CharSequence text) function to refresh the TextView display.

In Android, the accessor functions of a class attribute usually start with set/get, such as the read/write functions of the EditText contents:

```
Editable getText()
void setText(CharSequence text, TextView.BufferType type)
```

The interface of this application is shown in Figure 2-11; (a) is the start screen, (b) is the screen after text is entered in the edit text box, and (c) shows the application screen after the button is clicked.

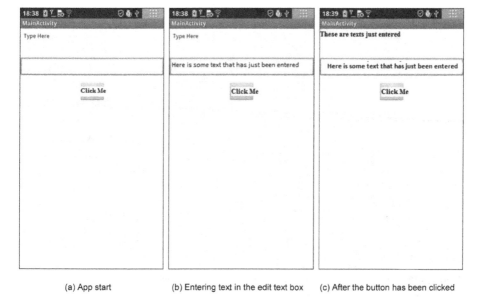

(a) App start   (b) Entering text in the edit text box   (c) After the button has been clicked

Figure 2-11. The interface of the application with a TextView, a Button, and an EditText

Using ImageView

Previous sections discussed typical uses of widgets and showed the basic concepts of widget programming. The image is the foundation of multimedia applications and is thus a major part of Android applications. This section introduces the use of the image/picture display widget, ImageView. Through the examples in this section, you learn how to use ImageView and add files to the project's resources.

The following example was originally developed in the section when you created the GuiExam application. Follow these steps to add a picture file to the project:

1. Copy the image file (in this case, morphing.png) into the corresponding /res/drawable-XXX project directory (the directory in which to store project files of different resolution images), as shown in Figure 2-12.

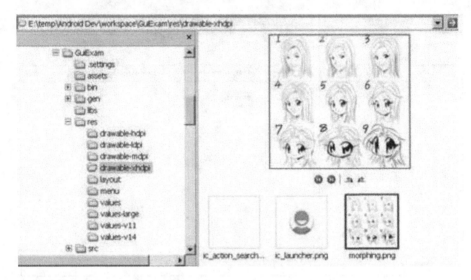

Figure 2-12. *Copy the image file into the project's* res *directory*

2. Open the project in Eclipse, and press the F5 key to refresh the project. You can see the file added to the project in Package Explorer (in this case, morphing.png), as shown in Figure 2-13.

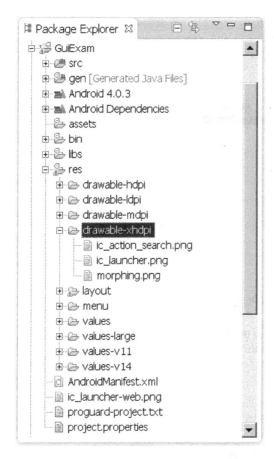

Figure 2-13. *The Package Explorer window after the image is added*

To place ImageView widgets in the layout, follow these steps:

1. Click to select the TextView widget of the "Hello world!" project, and then press the Del key to remove the widget from the layout.

2. In the editor window of layout.xml, locate the Image & Media branch, and drag and drop the ImageView of this branch to the layout file. When the Resource Chooser dialog box pops up, click and select the Project Resource, select the just-imported picture file under the project, and click OK to complete the operation. This process is shown in Figure 2-14.

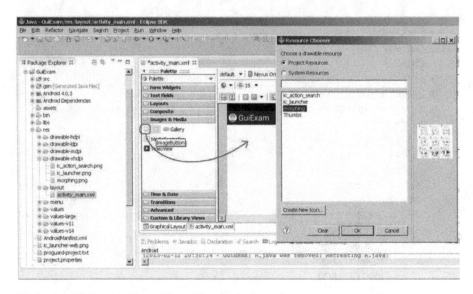

Figure 2-14. *Place the ImageView widget in the layout.*

3.   Adjust the size and position of the ImageView, and set its
      properties. This step can use the default values shown
      in Figure 2-15.

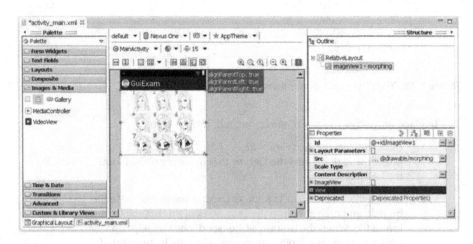

Figure 2-15. *The property settings of the ImageView*

4.   Save the layout file.

Normally, at this point, you would have to compile the Java code. However, in this
example, compiling is not necessary. Figure 2-16 shows the application's interface.

Figure 2-16. *Application interface of the* ImageView

Exit Activities and Application

In the previous example, you can press the phone's Back button to hide the activity, but doing so does not close the activity. As you saw in the section "State Transitions of Activities," when the Back button is pressed, started activities only change from the active state to the non-active state and remain in the system stack. To close these activities and remove them from the stack, you should use the finish function of the Activity class.

However, closing activities does not mean the application process ends. Even if all the components of the application (activity, service, broadcast intent receiver, and so on) are closed, the application process continues to exist. There are two main ways to exit the application process.

One is the static function System.exit that Java provides to forcibly end the process; another is the static function Process.killProcess (pid) provided by Android to terminate the specified process ID (PID). You can pass the Process.myPid() static function to get the application's process ID.

You can use these methods for the example in the section "Using ImageView." The specific steps are as follows:

1. Add two buttons to the layout file with the Text property "Close Activity" and "Exit Application" respectively and ID attributes @+id/closeActivity and @+id/exitApplication respectively. Adjust the buttons' size and position, as shown in Figure 2-17.

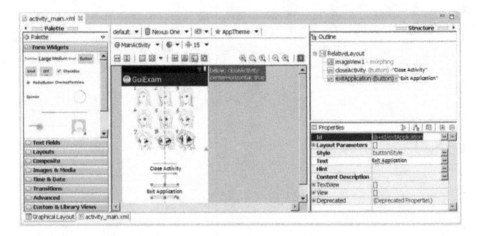

Figure 2-17. *Add Close Activity and Exit Application buttons in the layout*

2. Modify the source code of the MainActivity.java file as follows (the bold code is either added or modified, and the lines with strikethrough indicate deleted code):

```
Line #    Source Code
1 package com.example.guiexam;
2 import android.os.Bundle;
3 import android.app.Activity;
4 import android.view.Menu;
5 //import android.view.MenuItem;
6 //import android.support.v4.app.NavUtils;
7 import android.widget.Button;          //Use Button class
8 import android.view.View;              //Use View class
```

```
 9  import android.view.View.OnClickListener;
    // Use View.OnClickListenerClass
10  import android.os.Process;
    // Use killProcess method

11  public class MainActivity extends Activity {
12      @Override
13      public void onCreate(Bundle savedInstanceState) {
14          super.onCreate(savedInstanceState);
15          setContentView(R.layout.activity_main);
16          Button btn = (Button) findViewById(R.
            id.closeActivity);
17  // Get Button object of <Closed activity>
18          btn.setOnClickListener(new /*View.*/OnClickListener(){
19  // Set response code for Clicking
20              public void onClick(View v) {
21                  finish();
    // Close main activity
22              }
23          });
24          btn = (Button) findViewById(R.id.exitApplication);
25  // Get Button object of <Exit Application>
26  // Set the response code to Clicking
27              public void onClick(View v) {
28                  finish();
    // close main activity
29                  Process.killProcess(Process.myPid());
    // Exit application process

30              }
31
32
33
34
35          });
    }

    @Override
    public boolean onCreateOptionsMenu(Menu menu) {
        getMenuInflater().inflate(R.menu.activity_main, menu);
        return true;
    }
}
```

In lines 5 and 6, you remove the unused import statements. You set the response code for the Close Activity button in lines 16-21 and set the response code for the Exit Application button in lines 22-28. The only difference is that the latter adds the application-exit code Process.killProcess (Process.myPid ()). Both buttons use the same finish() function of the Activity class to close the activity. The code in lines 7-10 imports related classes.

The application interface is shown in Figure 2-18.

Figure 2-18. *The Close Activity and Exit Application interface of the application*

When you click the Close Activity or Exit Application button, the main interface of the application is turned off. The difference is that the application process (com.example. guiexam) does not quit for Close Activity; but for Exit Application, the process closes. This is clearly shown in the Devices pane of the DDMS view in Eclipse, in which you can see a list of processes on the target machine, as shown in Figure 2-19.

(a) Processes after clicking Close Activity   (b) Processes after clicking Exit Application

Figure 2-19. *The process in DDMS when the Close Activity and Exit Application application is running*

Summary

This chapter introduced Android interface design by having you create a simple application called GuiExam. You learned about the state transitions of activities, the Context class, intent, and the relationship between applications and activities. You also saw how to use the layout as an interface by changing the layout file activity_main. xml, and you saw how the button, event, and inner event listeners work. The next chapter describes how to create an application with multiple activities using the activity-intent mechanism and shows the changes needed in the AndroidManifest.xml file.

CHAPTER 3

GUI Design for Android Apps, Part 3: Designing Complex Applications

In the previous chapter, you learned about Android interface design by creating a simple application called GuiExam. The chapter also covered the state transition of activities, the Context class, and an introduction to intents and the relationship between applications and activities. You learned how to use a layout as an interface, and how button, event, and inner event listeners work. In this chapter, you learn how to create an application with multiple activities; examples introduce the explicit and implicit trigger mechanisms of activities. You see an example of an application with parameters triggered by an activity in a different application, which will help you understand the exchange mechanism for the activity's parameters.

Applications with Multiple Activities

The application in the previous example has only one activity: the main activity, which is displayed when the application starts. This chapter demonstrates an application with multiple activities, using the activity-intent mechanism, and shows the changes needed in the AndroidManifest.xml file.

As previously described, an activity is triggered by an intent. There are two kinds of intent-resolution methods: *explicit match* (also known as *direct intent*) and *implicit match* (also known as *indirect intent*). A triggering activity can also have parameters and return values. Additionally, Android comes with a number of built-in activities, and therefore a triggered activity can come from Android itself, or it can be customized. Based on these situations, this chapter uses four examples to illustrate different activities. For the explicit match, you see an application with or without parameters and return values. For the implicit match, you see an application that uses activities that come from the Android system or are user defined.

Triggering an Explicit Match of Activities with No Parameters

Using explicit match without parameters is the simplest trigger mechanism of the activity intent. This section first uses an example to introduce this mechanism and later covers more complex mechanisms.

The code framework of the activity-intent triggering mechanism for explicit matching includes two parts: the activities of the callee (being triggered) and those of the caller (trigger). The trigger is not limited to activities; it can also be a service, such as a broadcast intent receiver. But because you have only seen the use of activities so far, the triggers for all the examples in this section are activities.

1. The source code framework for the activity of the callee does the following:

    a. Defines a class that inherits from the activity.

    b. If there are parameters that need to be passed, then the source code framework of the activity calls the `Activity.getIntent()` function in the onCreate function to obtain the `Intent` object that triggers this activity, and then gets the parameters being passed through functions like `Intent.getData ()`, `Intent.getXXXExtra ()`, `Intent.getExtras ()`, and so on.

    c. Writes code for the normal activity patterns.

    d. If the trigger returns values, does the following before exiting the activity:

        i. Defines an `Intent` object

        ii. Sets data values for the intent with functions like `Intent.putExtras()`

        iii. Sets the return code of the activity by calling the `Activity.setResult()` function

    e. Adds the code for the activity of the callee in the `AndroidManifest.xml` file.

2. The code framework for the activity of the callee does the following:

    a. Defines the `Intent` object, and specifies the trigger's context and the `class` attribute of the triggered activity.

    b. If parameters need to be passed to the activity, sets the parameters for the `Intent` object by calling functions of the intent like `setData()`, `putExtras()`, and so on.

c. Calls `Activity.startActivity(Intent intent)` function to trigger an activity without parameters, or call `Activity.startActivityForResult(Intent intent, int requestCode)` to trigger an activity with parameters.

d. If the activity needs to be triggered by the return value, then the code framework rewrites the `onActivityResult()` function of the `Activity` class, which takes different actions depending on the request code (`requestCode`), result code (`resultCode`), and intentions (`Intent`) values.

In step 2a, the class attribute of the triggered activity is used, which involves a Java mechanism called *reflection*. This mechanism can create and return an object of the class according to the class name. The object of the triggered activity is not constructed before the triggering; therefore triggering the activity also means creating an object of that class so that subsequent operations can continue. That is, triggering the activity includes the operation of the newly created class objects.

The following two examples illustrate the code framework in detail. This section describes the first one. In this example, the triggered activity belongs to the same application as the activity of the trigger, and the triggered activity does not require any parameters and does not return any values. The new activity is triggered via a button, and its activity interface is similar to the interface of the example in the section "Exit Activities and Application." in Chapter 2, Figure 2-16. The entire application interface is shown in Figure 3-1.

(a) Interface when the app starts

(b) Interface when Change To The New Interface Without Parameters is clicked

(c) Interface when Close Activity is clicked

Figure 3-1. *The application interface with multiple activities in the same application without parameters*

73

After the application starts, the application's main activity is displayed, as shown in Figure 3-1(a). When the Change To The New Interface Without Parameters button is clicked, the app displays the new activity, as shown in Figure 3-1(b). Clicking the Close Activity button causes the interface to return to the application's main activity, as shown in Figure 3-1(c).

Create this example by modifying and rewriting the example in the GuiExam section in Chapter 2, as follows:

1. Generate the corresponding layout file for the triggered activity:

    a. Right-click the shortcut menu in the res\layout subdirectory of the application, and select New ➤ Other Items. A New dialog box pops up. Select the \XML\XML File subdirectory, and click Next to continue. In the New XML File dialog box, enter the file name (in this case noparam_otheract.xml), and click Finish. The entire process is shown in Figure 3-2.

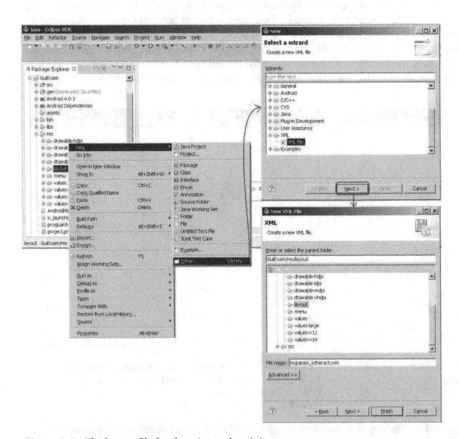

Figure 3-2. *The layout file for the triggered activity*

■ **Note**   The file name is the name of the layout file. You must use only lowercase letters for compilation to be successful; otherwise you will get the error "Invalid file name: must contain only a-z0-9_."

You can see the newly added xxx.xml file (in this case, noparam_otheract.xml) in the project's Package Explorer, as shown in Figure 3-3.

Figure 3-3. *Initial interface of the application's newly added layout file*

■ **Note**   The layout editor window on the right is still empty, and there is no visible interface so far.

b.   Select the Layouts subdirectory in the left palette, and drag the layout control (in this case, RelativeLayout) onto the window in the right pane. You immediately see a visible (phone-screen shaped) interface, as shown in Figure 3-4.

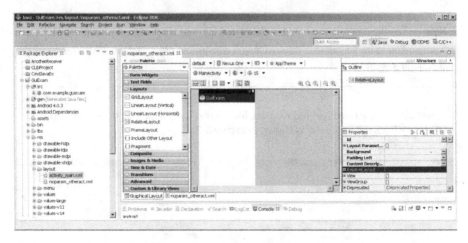

Figure 3-4. *Drag-and-drop layout for the newly added layout file*

     c.   Based on the same methodology described in the section "Using ImageView" in Chapter 2, place an ImageView and a button in the new layout file. Set the ImageView widget's ID attribute to @+id/picture and the Button widget's ID attribute to @+id/closeActivity. The Text property is "Close Activity," as shown in Figure 3-5. Finally, save the layout file.

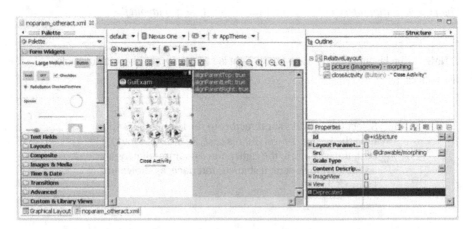

Figure 3-5. *Final configuration of the newly added layout file*

2. Add the corresponding `Activity` class for the layout file
   (Java source files). To do so, right-click `\src\com.example.XXX`
   under the project directory, and select New ➤ Class on the
   shortcut menu. In the New Java Class dialog box, for Name, enter
   the `Activity` class name corresponding to the new layout file
   (in this case, `TheNoParameterOtherActivity`). Click Finish to
   close the dialog box. The whole process is shown in Figure 3-6.

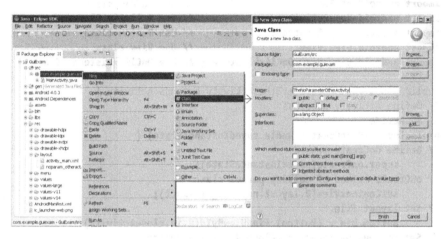

Figure 3-6. *Corresponding class for the newly added layout file*

You can see the newly added Java files (in this case, `TheNoParameterOtherActivity.java`) and the initial code, as shown in Figure 3-7.

Figure 3-7. *Corresponding class and initial source code of the newly added layout*

3. Edit the newly added .java file
    (TheNoParameterOtherActivity.java). This class executes
    the activity of the triggered activity (callee). Its source code is
    as follows (bold text is added or modified):

```
Line #          Source Code
1   package com.example.guiexam;
2   import android.os.Bundle;              // Use Bundle class
3   import android.app.Activity;           // Use Activity Class
4   import android.widget.Button;          // Use Button class
5   import android.view.View;              // Use View class
6   import android.view.View.OnClickListener; // Use OnClickListener Class

7   public class TheNoParameterOtherActivity extends Activity {
8   // Define Activity subclass
9       @Override
10  protected void onCreate(Bundle savedInstanceState) {
11  // Define onCreate method
12          super.onCreate(savedInstanceState);
13  // onCreate method of calling parent class
14          setContentView(R.layout.noparam_otheract);
15  // Set layout file
16          Button btn = (Button) findViewById(R.id.closeActivity);
17  // Set responding code for <Close Activity> Button
18          btn.setOnClickListener(new /*View.*/OnClickListener(){
19              public void onClick(View v) {
                    finish();
    // Close this activity
                }
            });
        }
    }
```

In line 7, you add the superclass Activity for the newly created class. The code
in lines 8 through 18 is similar to the application's main activity. Note that in line 14,
the code calls the setContentView() function to set the layout for Activity, where the
parameter is the prefix name of the new layout XML file created in the first step.

4. Edit the code for the trigger (caller) activity. The trigger
    activity is the main activity of the application. The source code
    is MainActivity.java, and the layout file is activity_main.xml.
    The steps for editing are as follows:

    a. Edit the layout file, delete the original TextView
        widgets, and add a button. Set its ID property to
        @+id/goTONoParamNewAct and its Text property to
        "Change to interface without Parameter," as shown in
        Figure 3-8.

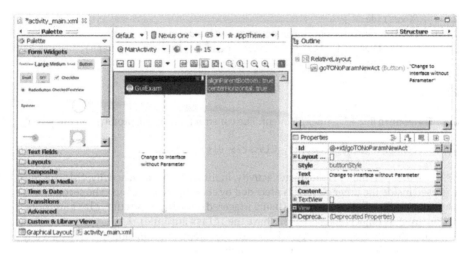

Figure 3-8. *Layout configuration for the trigger activity*

    b.   Edit the source code file of the trigger activity (in this
        case, MainActivity.java) as follows (bold text is either
        added or modified):

```
Line #        Source Code
1  package com.example.guiexam;
2  import android.os.Bundle;
3  import android.app.Activity;
4  import android.view.Menu;
5  import android.content.Intent;              // Use Intent class
6  import android.widget.Button;               // Use Button class
7  import android.view.View.OnClickListener;
8  import android.view.View;

9  public class MainActivity extends Activity {
10     @Override
11     public void onCreate(Bundle savedInstanceState) {
12         super.onCreate(savedInstanceState);
13         setContentView(R.layout.activity_main);
14     Button btn = (Button) findViewById(R.id.goTONoParamNewAct);
15     btn.setOnClickListener(new /*View.*/OnClickListener(){
16         public void onClick(View v) {
17             Intent intent = new Intent(MainActivity.this,
                                    TheNoParameterOtherActivity.class);
18             startActivity(intent);
19         }
20     });
21     }
```

```
22      @Override
23      public boolean onCreateOptionsMenu(Menu menu) {
24          getMenuInflater().inflate(R.menu.activity_main, menu);
25          return true;
26      }
27 }
```

The code in line 17 defines an intent. The constructor function prototype in this case is

```
Intent(Context packageContext, Class<?> cls)
```

The first parameter is the trigger activity, in this case the main activity; this, because it is used inside the inner classes, is preceded by class-name modifiers. The second parameter is the class of the callee (being triggered) activity. It uses the .class attribute to construct its object (all Java classes have the .class attribute).

Line 18 calls startActivity, which runs the intent. This function does not pass any parameters to the triggered activity. The function prototype is

```
void Activity.startActivity(Intent intent)
```

5. Edit the AndroidManifest.xml file. Add descriptive information for the callee activity (bold text is added) to register the new Activity class:

```
Line #          Source Code
1  <manifest xmlns:android="http://schemas.android.com/apk/res/android"
2      package="com.example.guiexam"
3      android:versionCode="1"
4      android:versionName="1.0" >
...    ... ...
10     <application
11         android:icon="@drawable/ic_launcher"
12         android:label="@string/app_name"
13         android:theme="@style/AppTheme" >
14         <activity
15             android:name=".MainActivity"
16             android:label="@string/title_activity_main" >
17             <intent-filter>
18                 <action android:name="android.intent.action.MAIN" />
19
20                 <category android:name="android.intent.category.LAUNCHER" />
21             </intent-filter>
22         </activity>
23         <activity android:name=".TheNoParameterOtherActivity"
                android:label="the other Activity"/>
24     </application>
25
26 </manifest>
```

You can also replace this XML code with the following methods:

- Method 1:

```
<activity android:name="TheNoParameterOtherActivity"
android:label=" the other Activity"> </activity>
```

- Method 2:

```
<activity android:name=".TheNoParameterOtherActivity " />
```

- Method 3:

```
<activity android:name=".TheNoParameterOtherActivity">
</activity>
```

The content of the android: name text field is the class name of the callee's activity: TheNoParameterOtherActivity.

Note that if a period (.) is added before the name of the Activity class android: name, the compiler will give you the following warning at this line in the XML file (only a warning, not a compile error):

```
Exported activity does not require permission
```

Triggering Explicit Matching of an Activity with Parameters of Different Applications

The previous sections introduced triggering another activity without parameters in the same application. The activity of the trigger is that the callee allows the exchange of parameters: the trigger can specify certain parameters to the callee, and the callee can return those parameter values to the trigger on exit. Additionally, the callee and the trigger can be in completely different applications. This section shows an example of an application with parameters triggered by an activity in a different application. This example will help you understand the exchange mechanism for the activity's parameters.

Use the same GuiExam application from Chapter 2. The interface is shown in Figure 3-9.

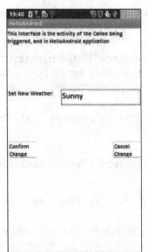

(a) Interface when the GuiExam application starts

(b) Interface after clicking Enter New Interface To Modify the Weather

(c) Entering a new value in the Set New Weather text box

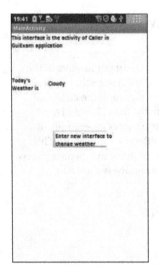

(d) Interface after clicking Confirm Change

(e) Interface after clicking Enter New Interface To Modify The Weather and entering a new value in the Set New Weather text box

(f) Interface after clicking Cancel Change

Figure 3-9. *The interface of multiple activities in different applications*

As shown in Figure 3-9, the trigger activity is in the GuiExam application, where there is a variable to accept the weather condition entry. The interface in Figure 3-9(a) displays when the GuiExam application is opened. Click the Enter New Interface To Modify The Weather box to trigger the activity in HelloAndroid. When this activity starts, it displays the new weather condition passed in the Set New Weather text box, as shown in Figure 3-9(b). Now enter a new weather condition value in the Set New Weather, and click OK Change to close the trigger's activity. The new value returned from Set New Weather refreshes the Weather variable in the trigger's activity, as shown in Figure 3-9(d). If you click Cancel Change, it does the same thing and closes the activity, but the value Weather does not change, as shown in Figure 3-9(f).

The process list for the executing application is shown in Figure 3-10 (displayed in the DDMS window of the host machine in Eclipse).

(a) When the GuiExam application starts

(b) After clicking Enter New Interface To Modify The Weather

(c) After clicking Confirm Change or Cancel Change

(d) After the GuiExam application exits

Figure 3-10. *Process list in DDMS for the multiple-activity application*

Figure 3-10 shows that when the application starts, only the process for the trigger, GuiExam, is running. But when you click Enter New Interface To Modify The Weather, the new activity is triggered and the process for the new activity HelloAndroid runs, as shown in Figure 3-10(b). When you click Confirm Change or Cancel Change, the triggered activity turns off, but the HelloAndroid process does not quit, as shown in Figure 3-10(c). Interestingly, even though the GuiExam trigger process exits, the HelloAndroid process to which the triggered activity belongs is still in the running state.

The build steps are as follows:

1. Modify the GuiExam code of the trigger application:

    a. Edit the main layout file (activity_main.xml in this case) by deleting the original TextView widgets; then add three new TextView widgets and a button. Set their properties as follows: set the Text property for two TextViews to "This interface is the activity of the Caller in GuiExam application" and "Today's Weather:". Set the third TextView's ID property to @+id/weatherInfo. The Text property of the button is "Enter New Interface to Change Weather", and its ID attribute is @+id/modifyWeather. Adjust the size and position of each widget as shown in Figure 3-11.

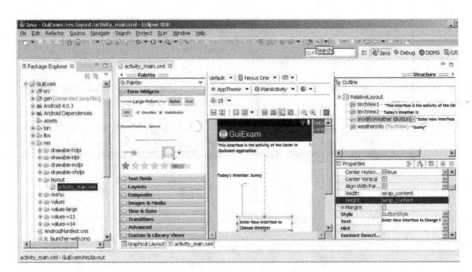

Figure 3-11. *The main layout design for the GuiExam trigger application*

b.   Modify the content of `MainActivity.java` as shown here:

```
Line#        Source Code
1  package com.example.guiexam;
2  import android.os.Bundle;
3  import android.app.Activity;
4  import android.view.Menu;
5  import android.widget.Button;              // Use Button class
6  import android.view.View;                  // Use View class
7  import android.view.View.OnClickListener;  // Use View.OnClickListener class
8  import android.widget.TextView;            // Use TextView class
9  import android.content.Intent;             // Use Intentclass

10 public class MainActivity extends Activity {
11     public static final String INITWEATHER = "Sunny; // /Initial Weather
12     public static final int MYREQUESTCODE =100;
13 //Request Code of triggered Activity
14     private TextView tv_weather;
15 // The TextView Widget that displays Weather info
16     @Override
17     public void onCreate(Bundle savedInstanceState) {
18         super.onCreate(savedInstanceState);
19         setContentView(R.layout.activity_main);
20     tv_weather = (TextView)findViewById(R.id.weatherInfo);
21     tv_weather.setText(INITWEATHER);
22     Button btn = (Button) findViewById(R.id.modifyWeather);
23 //Get Button object according to resource ID #
24     btn.setOnClickListener(new /*View.*/OnClickListener(){
25 //Set responding code click event
26         public void onClick(View v) {
27             Intent intent = new Intent();
28             intent.setClassName("com.example.helloandroid",
29 // the package ( application) that the triggered Activity is located
30             "com.example.helloandroid.TheWithParameterOtherActivity");
31 //triggered class ( full name)
               String wthr = tv_weather.getText().toString();
32 // Acquire the value of weather TextView
               intent.putExtra("weather",wthr); // Set parameter being
33                                                    passed to Activity
34             startActivityForResult(intent, MYREQUESTCODE);
35 //Trigger Activity
36         }
37     });
38 }
```

```
39
40     @Override
41     protected void onActivityResult(int requestCode, int resultCode,
                            Intent data) {
42 //Triggered Activity finish return
43          super.onActivityResult(requestCode, resultCode, data);
44          if (requestCode == MYREQUESTCODE) {
45 // Determine whether the specified Activity end of the run
             if (resultCode == RESULT_CANCELED)
46                  {       }
47 // Select "Cancel" to exit the code, this case is empty
48                  else if (resultCode == RESULT_OK) {
49 // Select <OK> to exit code
50                      String wthr = null;
51                      wthr = data.getStringExtra("weather");
   // Get return value
                     if (wthr != null)
                          tv_weather.setText(wthr);
   // Update TextView display of weather content
                 }
             }
         }

     @Override
     public boolean onCreateOptionsMenu(Menu menu) {
         getMenuInflater().inflate(R.menu.activity_main, menu);
         return true;
     }
}
```

The code in lines 23–28 triggers the activity with parameters in other applications. Lines 23–25 establish the trigger intent, which uses the Intent.setClassName() function. The prototype is

```
Intent Intent.setClassName(String packageName, String className);
```

The first parameter is the name of the package where the triggered activity is located, and the second parameter is the class name (required to use the full name) of the triggered activity. By using the startActivity ... function to trigger the activity, the system can accurately locate the application and activity classes.

Line 28 attaches the parameter as additional data to the intent. Intent has a series of putExtra functions to attach additional data and another series of getXXXExtra functions to extract data from the intent. Additional data can also be assembled by the Bundle class. Intent provides a putExtras function to add data and a getExtras function to get the data. putExtra uses a *property-value* data pairing or *variable name-value* data pairing to add and retrieve data. In this example, Intent.putExtra("weather", "XXX") saves the data pair consisting of the name of the weather variable and the value "XXX" as additional data for the intent.

The code line with Intent.getStringExtra("weather") gets the value of the weather variable from the attached intent data and returns the string type.

More details about these functions and the Bundle class can be found in the documentation on the Android web site. They are not discussed any further here.

In lines 33–46, you rewrite the onActivityResult function of the Activity class. This function is called when the triggered activity is closed. In line 36, you first determine which activity is closed and returned according to the request code. Then you judge whether it is returned by an OK or a Cancel click, based on the result code and the request code. Lines 40–50 get the negotiated variable values from the returned intent. Line 42 updates the interface based on the return value of the variable. In this function, if the user clicks Cancel to return, you do nothing.

2. Modify the code of the callee application HelloAndroid as shown in Figure 3-12:

   a. Using the method described in the section "Triggering Explicit Matching of an Activity with Parameters of Different Applications earlier in this chapter, add a layout file (in this case named param_otheract.xml), and drag and drop a RelativeLayout layout into the file.

   b. Edit this layout file by adding two TextView widgets, an EditText, and two Button widgets. Set their properties as follows:

      • Text property for the two TextView widgets: "This interface is the activity of the caller in HelloAndroid application" and "Set new weather as:"

      • ID property for the EditText: @+id/editText_NewWeather

      • Text property for the two Buttons: "Confirm Changes" and "Cancel Changes"

      • ID attribute for the two Buttons: @+id/button_Modify and @+id/button_Cancel

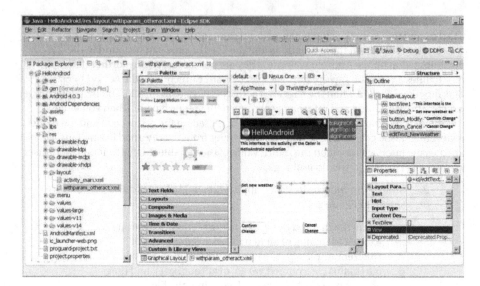

Figure 3-12. *New layout design of the triggered (callee) application* `HelloAndroid`

Then adjust their size and position.

c. As described in the section "Triggering Explicit Matching of an Activity with Parameters of Different Applications," add the corresponding class (in this case, `TheWithParameterOtherActivity`) for the new layout file, as shown in Figure 3-13.

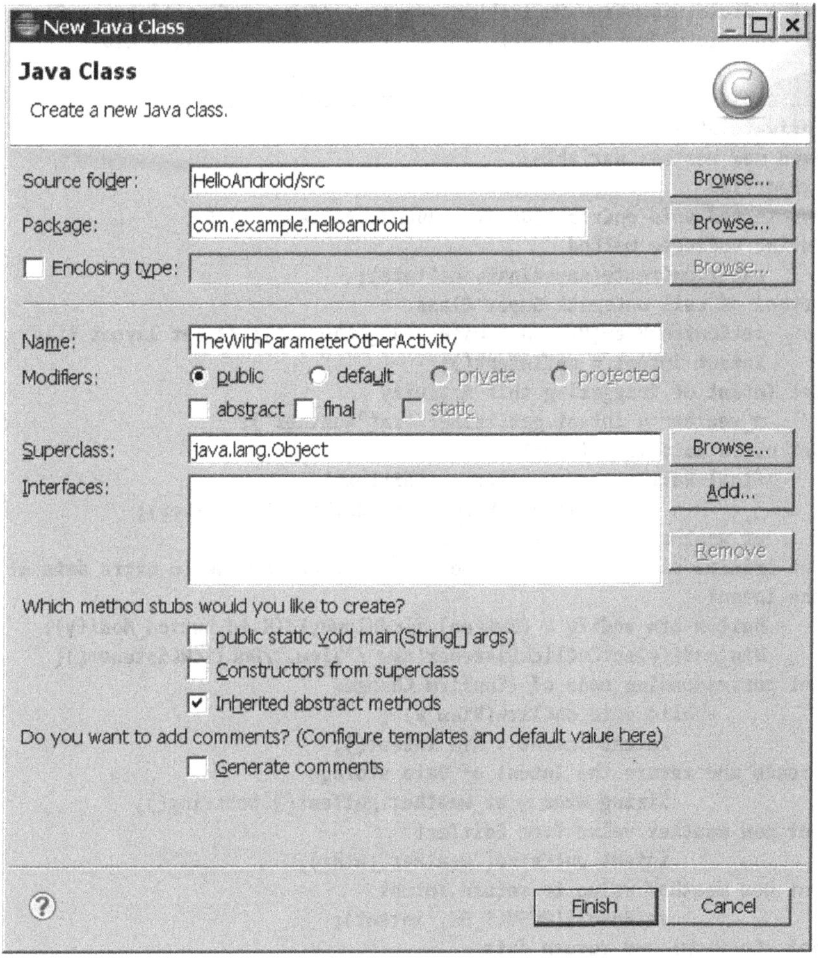

Figure 3-13. *Add the corresponding class for the newly added layout file in the* HelloAndroid *project*

d. Edit the class file for the newly added layout file
(in this example, TheWithParameterOtherActivity.java).
The content is as follows:

```
Line#        Source Code
1  package com.example.helloandroid;
2  import android.os.Bundle;            // Use Bundle Class
3  import android.app.Activity;         // Use Activity Class
4  import android.content.Intent;       // Use Intent Class
5  import android.widget.Button;        // Use Button Class
6  import android.view.View;            // Use View Class
```

```
7  import android.view.View.OnClickListener;     // Use OnClickListener Class
8  import android.widget.EditText;               // Use  EditText Class

9  public class TheWithParameterOtherActivity extends Activity {
10     private String m_weather;
11 // Save new weather variable
12     @Override
13     protected void onCreate(Bundle savedInstanceState) {
14 // Define onCreate method
15         super.onCreate(savedInstanceState);
16 // method of call onCreate Super Class
17         setContentView(R.layout.withparam_otheract); // Set layout file
18         Intent intent = getIntent();
19 // Get Intent of triggering this Activity
20         m_weather = intent.getStringExtra("weather");
21 // Get extra data from Intent
22         final EditText et_weather = (EditText)
                            findViewById(R.id.editText_NewWeather);
23         et_weather.setText(m_weather,null);
24 // Set initial value of "New Weather" EditText according to extra data of
   the Intent
25         Button btn_modify = (Button) findViewById(R.id.button_Modify);
26         btn_modify.setOnClickListener(new /*View.*/OnClickListener(){
27 // Set corresponding code of <Confirm Change>
28             public void onClick(View v) {
29                 Intent intent = new Intent();
30 // Create and return the Intent of Data storage
31                 String wthr = et_weather.getText().toString();
32 // Get new weather value from EditText
33                 intent.putExtra("weather",wthr);
34 // Put new weather value to return Intent
35                 setResult(RESULT_OK, intent);
36 // Set <Confirm> and return data
37                 finish(); // Close Activity
            }
        });
        Button btn_cancel = (Button) findViewById(R.id.button_Cancel);
        btn_cancel.setOnClickListener(new /*View.*/OnClickListener(){
// Set corresponding code for <Cancel Change>
            public void onClick(View v) {
                setResult(RESULT_CANCELED, null);
// Set return value for <Cancel>
                finish(); // Close this Activity
            }
        });
    }
}
```

This code follows the framework of an activity. It sets the activity layout in line 11 such that the layout name is the same.as the layout file name created in step 1 (no extension). In lines 19–22, it first constructs an intent for the return and then adds extra data to the Intent object as the return data. In line 21, it sets the return value of the activity and the intent as a return data carrier. The prototype of the setResult function is

```
final void Activity.setResult(int resultCode, Intent data);
```

If resultCode is RESULT_OK, the user has clicked OK to return; and if it is RESULT_CANCELLED, the user has clicked Cancel to return. In this condition, the return data carrier intent can be null, which is set in line 27.

3. Modify AndroidManifest.xml, which is triggered by the application, with the following code:

```
Line #          Source Code
1   <manifest xmlns:android="http://schemas.android.com/apk/res/android"
2       package="com.example.helloandroid"
3       android:versionCode="1"
4       android:versionName="1.0" >
5
6       <uses-sdk
7           android:minSdkVersion="8"
8           android:targetSdkVersion="15" />
9
10      <application
11          android:icon="@drawable/ic_launcher"
12          android:label="@string/app_name"
13          android:theme="@style/AppTheme" >
14          <activity
15              android:name=".MainActivity"
16              android:label="@string/title_activity_main" >
17              <intent-filter>
18                  <action android:name="android.intent.action.MAIN" />
19
20                  <category android:name="android.intent.category.LAUNCHER" />
21              </intent-filter>
22          </activity>
23          <activity
24              android:name="TheWithParameterOtherActivity">
25              <intent-filter>
26                  <action android:name="android.intent.action.DEFAULT" />
27              </intent-filter>
28          </activity>
29      </application>
30
31  </manifest>
```

4.   Lines 24–29 are new. As in previous sections, you add an additional activity description and specify its class name, which is the class name of the triggered activity generated in the second step. See the section "Triggering an Explicit Match of Activities with No Parameters" for information about modifying the AndroidManifest.xml file. Unlike in that section, you add not only an activity and the documentation of its name attribute, but also the intent-filter instructions and state to accept the default actions described in the Action element and trigger this Activity class. The activity cannot be activated in the absence of the intent-filter description of the activity.

5.   Run the callee application to register components of the activity. The modifications to AndroidManifest.xml file are not registered to the Android system until the callee application, HelloAndroid, is executed once. Thus this is an essential step to complete the registration of its included activity.

Implicit Matching of Built-In Activities

In the examples in the previous two sections, before you trigger the activity of the same application or different applications through the Activity.startActivity() function or the Activity.startActivityForResult() function, the constructor of the Intent objects explicitly specifies the class, either through the .class attribute or through the class name in a string. This way, the system can find the class to be triggered. This approach is called *explicit intent matching*. The next example shows how to trigger a class that is not specified. Instead, the system figures it out using an approach called *implicit intent matching*.

In addition, Android has a number of activities that have already been implemented, such as dialing, sending text messages, and so on. Examples in this section explain how you use can implicit matching to trigger these built-in activities. The application interface is shown in Figure 3-14.

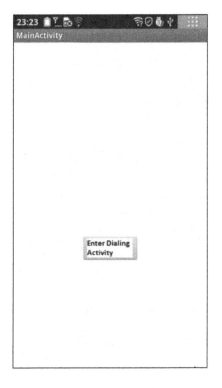 

(a) Application's start interface

(b) Interface after clicking Enter Dialing Activity

Figure 3-14. *The application interface when using implicit intent to trigger a built-in activity*

The user start the GuiExam application and clicks the Enter Dialing Activity button on the screen. It triggers dial-up activities that come with the system.

In this case, you modify the GuiExam project and use this application as a trigger. The implicit match triggered activity is the dial-up activity. The steps to build this example are as follows.

1.   In the layout file (activity_main.xml) of the GuiExam application, delete the original TextView widgets, add a button, and set its ID attribute to @+id/goTODialAct and its Text property to "Enter Dialing Activity". Adjust its size and position as shown in Figure 3-15.

Figure 3-15. *Layout file of the application for the implicit match built-in activity*

2. Modify the source code file (MainActivity.java) as follows:

```
Line#         Source Code
1  package com.example.guiexam;
2  import android.os.Bundle;
3  import android.app.Activity;
4  import android.view.Menu;
5  import android.widget.Button;            // Use Button Class
6  import android.view.View;                // Use View Class
7  import android.view.View.OnClickListener; // Use View.OnClickListener Class
8  import android.content.Intent;           // Use Intent Class
9  import android.net.Uri;                  // Use URI Class

10 public class MainActivity extends Activity {
11     @Override
12     public void onCreate(Bundle savedInstanceState) {
13         super.onCreate(savedInstanceState);
14         setContentView(R.layout.activity_main);
15         Button btn = (Button) findViewById(R.id.goTODialAct);
16         btn.setOnClickListener(new /*View.*/OnClickListener(){
17 // Set corresponding Code for Click Activity
18             public void onClick(View v) {
19                 Intent intent = new Intent(Intent.ACTION_DIAL,
                     Uri.parse("tel:13800138000"));
```

94

```
20              startActivity(intent); // Trigger corresponding Activity
21         }
22     });
   }
23
24     @Override
25     public boolean onCreateOptionsMenu(Menu menu) {
26         getMenuInflater().inflate(R.menu.activity_main, menu);
27         return true;
28     }
 }
```

The code in line 16 defines an *indirect intent* (that is, intent of implicit match. It is called an indirect intent because the class that needs to be triggered is not specified in the constructor of the object; the constructor only describes the function of the class that needs to be triggered to complete dialing. The constructor functions for the indirect intent are as follows:

```
Intent(String action)
Intent(String action, Uri uri)
```

These functions require the classes (activities) that can complete the specified action when they are called. The only difference between the two is that the second function also comes with data.

This example uses the second constructor, which requires the activity that can complete the dialing and extra data as a string of phone numbers. Because the application does not specify the trigger type, Android finds the class to handle this action (for example, Activity) from the registered class list and triggers the start of the event.

If multiple classes can handle the specified action, Android pops up a selection menu, and users can select which one to run.

The parameter action can use the system-predefined string. In the previous example, Intent.ACTION_DIAL is the string constant of ACTION_DIAL, which is defined by the Intent class. Some system-predefined ACTION examples are shown in Table 3-1.

Table 3-1. *Some System-Predefined* ACTION *Constants*

ACTION Constant Name	Value	Description
ACTION_MAIN	android.intent. action.MAIN	Start up as the initial activity of a task with no data input and no returned output.
ACTION_VIEW	android.intent. action.VIEW	Display the data in the intent URI.
ACTION_EDIT	android.intent. action.EDIT	Request an activity to edit data.
ACTION_DIAL	android.intent. action.DIAL	Start a phone dialer, and use preset numbers in the data to dial.
ACTION_CALL	android.intent. action.CALL	Initiate a phone call, and immediately use the number in the data URI to initiate a call.
ACTION_SEND	android.intent. action.SEND	Start an activity to send specific data (the recipient is selected by activity resolution).
ACTION_SENDTO	android.intent. action.SENDTO	Generally, start an activity to send a message to a contact designated in the URI.
ACTION_ANSWER	android.intent. action.ANSWER	Open an activity to process an incoming call. Currently it is handled by a local phone-dialing tool.
ACTION_INSERT	android.intent. action.INSERT	Open an activity that can insert a new project at the addition cursor in a specific data field. When it is called as the child activity, it must return the URI of the newly inserted project.
ACTION_DELETE	android.intent. action.DELETE	Start an activity to delete a data port at the URI position.
ACTION_WEB_SEARCH	android.intent. action.WEB_SEARCH	Open an activity, and run a web page search based on the text in the URI data.

The ACTION constant name is the first parameter used in the constructor of the implicit-match intent. The value of the ACTION constant, used in the AndroidManifest.xml statement of the activity that receives this action, is not used in this section, but is used in the next section. You can find more information about predefined ACTION values in the android.content.Intent help documentation.

Implicit Match that Uses a Custom Activity

The previous example used implicit matching to trigger activities that come with the Android system. In this section, you see an example of how to use an implicit match to trigger a custom activity.

The configuration of this example application is similar to the one in the section "Triggering Explicit Matching of an Activity with Parameters of Different Applications." The triggering application is hosted in the GuiExam project, and the custom activity triggered by implicit match is in the HelloAndroid application. The interface is shown in Figure 3-16.

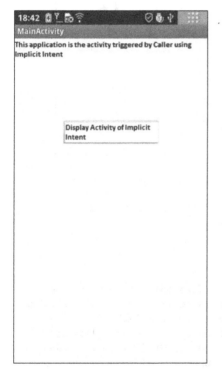

(a) Application's start interface

(b) Interface after clicking Display Activity Of Implicit Intent

Figure 3-16. *The interface of implicit match that uses a custom activity*

97

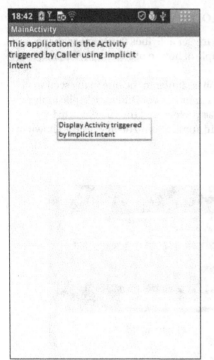

c) Interface after selecting HelloAndroid   (d) Interface after clicking Close Activity

Figure 3-16. (*continued*)

Figure 3-16(a) shows the interface when the GuiExam trigger application starts. When you click the Display Activity Of Implicit Intent button, the system finds qualified candidates for activities according to the requirements of the ACTION_EDIT action and displays a list of events of these candidates (b). When the user-defined HelloAndroid application is selected, the activity that can receive the ACTION_EDIT action as claimed in the intent-filter in HelloAndroid application is displayed (c). When you click the Close Activity button, the application returns to the original GuiExam activity interface (d).

Like the previous ones, this example is based on modifying the GuiExam project. The steps are as follows:

1. Edit the main layout file (activity_main.xml). Delete the original TextView widgets, and then add a TextView and a button. Set the TextView's Text property to "This application is the Activity triggered by Caller using Implicit Intent". Set the button's Text property to "Display Activity triggered by Implicit Intent" and its ID attribute to @+id/goToIndirectAct, as shown in Figure 3-17.

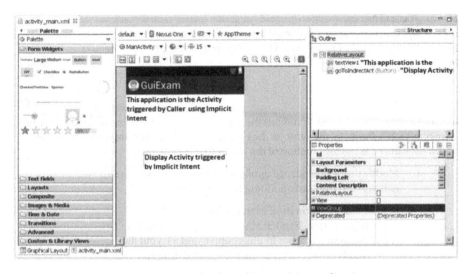

Figure 3-17. *The main layout design for the GuiExam trigger application*

2. Edit MainActivity.java as follows:

```
Line#       Source Code
1   package com.example.guiexam;
2   import android.os.Bundle;
3   import android.app.Activity;
4   import android.view.Menu;
5   import android.widget.Button;          // Use Button Class
6   import android.view.View;              // Use View class
7   import android.view.View.OnClickListener; // Use View.OnClickListener class
8   import android.content.Intent;         // Use Intent Class

9   public class MainActivity extends Activity {
10      @Override
11      public void onCreate(Bundle savedInstanceState) {
12          super.onCreate(savedInstanceState);
13          setContentView(R.layout.activity_main);
14          Button btn = (Button) findViewById(R.id.goToIndirectAct);
15          btn.setOnClickListener(new /*View.*/OnClickListener(){
16  // Set respond Code for Button Click event
17              public void onClick(View v) {
18                  Intent intent = new Intent(Intent.ACTION_EDIT);
19  //Construct implicit Inent
20                  startActivity(intent); // Trigger Activity
21              }
        });
22      }
23
```

```
24      @Override
25      public boolean onCreateOptionsMenu(Menu menu) {
26          getMenuInflater().inflate(R.menu.activity_main, menu);
27          return true;
        }
    }
```

The code in lines 16 and 17 defines the implicit intent and triggers the corresponding activity, which is basically the same as the earlier code that triggers implicit activity, but here it uses the constructor function of the intent that has no data.

3. Modify the HelloAndroid application that includes a custom activity with the corresponding implicit intent:

a. Based on the method described in the section "Triggering an Explicit Match of Activities with No Parameters," earlier in this chapter, add a layout file (implicit_act.xml) to the project and drag and drop a RelativeLayout layout into the file.

b. Edit the layout file, and add TextView, ImageView, and Button widgets. Set the attributes as follows:

- Text property of the TextView: "This interface is an Activity of the HelloAndroid, which is responsible for action triggered by the ACTION_EDIT"

- ImageView: Set up exactly as in the section "Using ImageView" in Chapter 2.

- Text property of the Button: "Close Activity"

- ID property of the Button: @+id/closeActivity.

Then adjust their respective size and position, as shown in Figure 3-18.

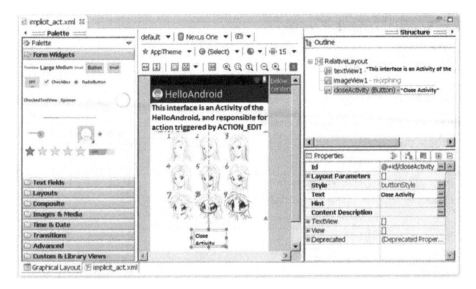

Figure 3-18. *Layout file for the custom activity of the corresponding implicit intent*

4. Similar to the process described in the section of this chapter "Triggering an Explicit Match of Activities with No Parameters," add the corresponding class to the project for the new layout file (`TheActivityToImplicitIntent`), as shown in Figure 3-19.

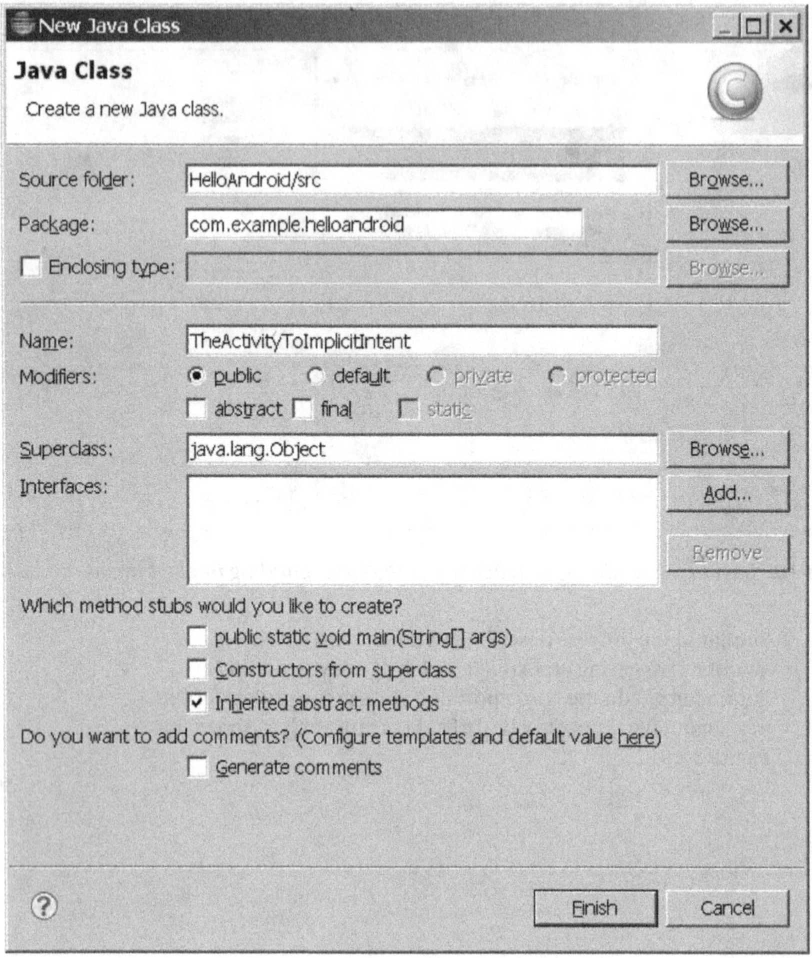

Figure 3-19. New class for the custom activity of the corresponding implicit intent

5. Edit the class file for the newly added layout file
   (TheActivityToImplicitIntent.java), which reads
   as follows:

```
Line#        Source Code
1   package com.example.helloandroid;
2   import android.os.Bundle;
3   import android.app.Activity;
4   import android.widget.Button;           // Use Button Class
5   import android.view.View;               // Use View class
6   import android.view.View.OnClickListener; // Use View.OnClickListener class
```

```
7   public class TheActivityToImplicitIntent extends Activity {
8   @Override
9   public void onCreate(Bundle savedInstanceState) {
10          super.onCreate(savedInstanceState);
11          setContentView(R.layout.implicit_act);
12          Button btn = (Button) findViewById(R.id.closeActivity);
13          btn.setOnClickListener(new /*View.*/OnClickListener(){
14  // Set response code for <Close Activity> Click
15              public void onClick(View v) {
16                  finish();
17              }
18          });
19      }
    }
```

6. Modify the AndroidManifest.xml file of the HelloAndroid custom application containing the corresponding implicit intent, as follows:

```
Line#       Source Code
1   <manifest xmlns:android="http://schemas.android.com/apk/res/android"
2
3       package="com.example.helloandroid"
4
5       android:versionCode="1"
6
7       android:versionName="1.0" >
8
9       <uses-sdk
10          android:minSdkVersion="8"
11          android:targetSdkVersion="15" />
12
13      <application
14          android:icon="@drawable/ic_launcher"
15          android:label="@string/app_name"
16          android:theme="@style/AppTheme" >
17          <activity
18              android:name=".MainActivity"
19              android:label="@string/title_activity_main" >
20              <intent-filter>
21                  <action android:name="android.intent.action.MAIN" />
22
23                  <category android:name="android.intent.category.LAUNCHER" />
24              </intent-filter>
25          </activity>
```

```
26        <activity
27            android:name="TheActivityToImplicitIntent">
28            <intent-filter>
29                <action android:name="android.intent.action.DEFAULT" />
30                <action android:name="android.intent.action.EDIT" />
31                <category android:name="android.intent.category.DEFAULT" />
32            </intent-filter>
33        </activity>
      </application>

</manifest>
```

The code in lines 24–32 (in bold) gives the activity information for receiving the implicit intent. Line 26 specifies that you can receive an android.intent.action.EDIT action. This value corresponds to the constant value of the ACTION parameter Intent.ACTION_EDIT of the trigger's intent constructor function (the MainActivity class of GuiExam). This is a predetermined contact signal between the trigger and the callee. Line 27 further specifies that the default data type can also be received.

7.   Run the application HelloAndroid, which now contains a custom activity for the corresponding implicit intent and registers its AndroidManifest.xml file in the system.

So far, three chapters have covered Android interface design. The simple GuiExam application has demonstrated the state transition of an activity, the Context class, intents, and the relationship between applications and activities. You also learned how to use a layout as an interface and how the button, event, and inner event listener work. Examples with multiple activities introduced the explicit and implicit trigger mechanisms for activities. You saw an example of an application with parameters triggered by an activity in a different application, and you now understand the exchange mechanism for the activity's parameters.

The application interface discussed so far is basically similar to a dialog interface. The drawback of this mode is that it is difficult to obtain accurate touchscreen input, making it difficult to display accurate images based on the input interface. The next chapter, which covers the last part of Android interface design, introduces the view-based interaction style interface. In this interface, you can enter information with accurate touchscreen input and display detailed images, as required by many game applications.

■ ■ ■

CHAPTER 4

GUI Design for Android Apps, Part 4: Graphic Interface and Touchscreen Input

So far, three chapters have been devoted to Android interface design. The application interface discussed so far is similar to a dialog interface. The drawback is that it is difficult to obtain accurate touchscreen input information, so it is hard to display accurate images based on the input interface. This chapter introduces the view-based interaction style interface. In this mode, you can enter information with accurate touchscreen input and display detailed images, which happen to be requirements for lots of game applications.

Display Output Framework

Unlike the dialog box–style interface, which consists of TextView, EditText, Button, and other window components, an interactive UI display directly uses a View class. This section introduces the basic framework of drawing in the view (that is, displaying images or graphics).

To display images and graphics in a view, you need to put drawing code into its onDraw function. The onDraw function is called whenever images need to be redrawn in a view, such as when the view is displayed when the application starts, when the front cover object (such as a view, an event, or a dialog box) on top of the graphic view is moved away, when the view from the bottom layer is moved into the top layer with the activity, or in similar circumstances. You're advised to put the drawing code in the View.onDraw function, so you can ensure when the view needs to be displayed to the user. The view window can also immediately be displayed in its total output; otherwise, certain graphic view areas may not be refreshed or repainted.

Android drawing functions such as draw rectangle, draw oval, draw straight line, and display text are usually integrated into the Canvas class. When the View.onDraw callback executes, it brings with it a Canvas parameter that is used to get the Canvas object.

105

Android uses the Paint class to draw a variety of graphics. Paint contains a variety of brush attributes, such as color, fill style, font, and font size.

As described earlier in the book, the interface configuration style of the application code generated in Eclipse is as follows: an activity includes layouts, and a layout contains two layers of widget structures. For this reason, you set parameters for the setContentView function in the onCreate function of the activity as the layout to achieve this effect. To use the view-based interface, you need to change the default parameter layout of the setContentView function to a custom view class.

Here is an example that illustrates the process. Modify the GuiExam example project by using the following steps:

1. Using the same steps as in the section "Triggering an Explicit Match of Activities with No Parameters" in Chapter 3, create a new class (MyView), as shown in Figure 4-1.

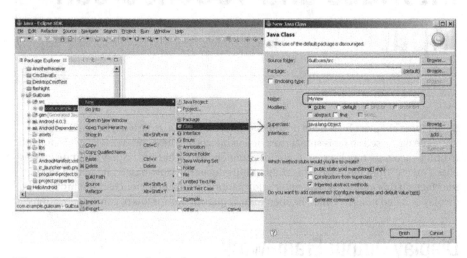

Figure 4-1. *Create a new class in the project*

2. Edit the source code of the newly added class (MyView.java). The content is shown next.

```
Line#          Source Code
1 package com.example.guiexam;
2
3 import android.view.View;
4 import android.graphics.Canvas;
5 import android.graphics.Paint;
6 import android.content.Context;

7 import android.graphics.Color;
8 import android.graphics.Paint.Style;
9 import android.graphics.Rect;
```

```
10 import android.graphics.Bitmap;
11 import android.graphics.BitmapFactory;
12 import android.graphics.Typeface;

13 public class MyView extends View {
14     MyView(Context context) {
15         super(context);
16     }

17     @Override
18     public void onDraw(Canvas canvas) {
19     Paint paint = new Paint();
20     paint.setAntiAlias(true); //  Sett anti-aliasing
21 // paint.setColor(Color.BLACK);  // Set Color Black
22 // paint.setStyle(Style.FILL);  // Set Fill Style
23     canvas.drawCircle(250, 250, 120, paint); // Draw Circle

24     paint.setColor(Color.RED); // Set color red
25     paint.setStyle(Style.STROKE); // Set style-Stroke ( no fill)
26     canvas.drawRect(new Rect(10, 10, 120, 100), paint); // draw rect

27     paint.setColor(0xff0000ff /*Color.BLUE*/ );
28     String str = "Hello!";
29     canvas.drawText(str, 150, 20, paint);        // display text

30     paint.setTextSize(50); // Set Text Size
31     paint.setTypeface(Typeface.SERIF);     // Set Typeface: Serif
32     paint.setUnderlineText(true); // Set Underline Text
33     canvas.drawText(str, 150, 70, paint);        // Display text

    Bitmap bitmap = BitmapFactory.
    decodeResource(getResources(),R.drawable.ic_launcher);
    canvas.drawBitmap(bitmap, 0, 250, paint);   // Display image
        }
    }
```

The code in line 13 adds extends View, which makes a custom class; in this case, MyView inherits from the View category. Lines 13–16 create a custom class constructor function that calls the superclass. This constructor function is essential to prevent the following compilation error:

```
Implicit super constructor View() is undefined. Must explicitly invoke
another constructor
```

Lines 17–34 override the View.onDraw function to program various pieces of drawing code. You construct a brush—that is, a Paint object—for drawing in line 16, and you set it to eliminate jagged edges in line 17. Line 23 draws a circle (x = 250, y = 250); line 24 sets the brush color to red, and so forth.

The prototype of the setColor function is

```
void Paint.setColor(int color);
```

In Android, a four-byte integer is used to represent a color, based on α, red, green, and blue. This integer data format looks like this:

$\alpha\alpha$	rr	gg	bb

From left to right, the first four bytes represent α, red, green, and blue values. For example, blue is 0xff0000ff, as is also reflected in line 27. In addition, the Android Color class also defines a constant for some colors, such as BLACK, RED, GREEN, BLUE, and so on, as reflected in line 24.

The setStyle function sets the fill mode of the brush. The function prototype is

```
void Paint.setStyle(Paint.Style style)
```

The parameter style can take Paint.Style.STROKE (hollow fill), Paint.Style.FILL (filled), or Paint.Style.FILL_AND_STROKE (solid and filled). These values are constants defined in the Paint.Style class; their corresponding display styles are shown in Table 4-1.

Table 4-1. Fill Mode Parameters and Examples

Image Displayed	Graphic Function Parameter Setting
	Color=BLACK, Style=FILL
	Color=BLACK, Style=STROKE
	Color=BLACK, Style=FILL_AND_STROKE

3. Modify the main Activity class (MainActivity.java) as follows:

```
Line#           Source Code
1 package com.example.guiexam;
2 import android.os.Bundle;
3 import android.app.Activity;
4 import android.view.Menu;
5 public class MainActivity extends Activity {
6     @Override
7     public void onCreate(Bundle savedInstanceState) {
8         super.onCreate(savedInstanceState);
9 //        setContentView(R.layout.activity_main);
10        setContentView(new MyView(this));
11 }
12 ......
```

The system automatically overrides the code in line 7 with the code in line 8. This allows a custom view class instead of the default layout as the interface of the activity.

The application interface is as shown in Figure 4-2; (a) shows the entire interface, and (b) is the enlarged section of the graphical display.

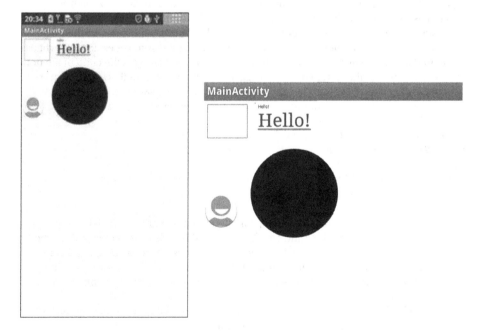

(a) Application's full UI   (b) Enlarged section of the application UI

Figure 4-2. *The interface of the display output framework of the GuiExam application*

109

Drawing Framework for Responding to Touchscreen Input

The previous example application only displays images/graphics and cannot respond to touchscreen input. In this section, you see how to respond to touchscreen input and control the view display.

View has an onTouchEvent function with the following function prototype:

```
boolean View.onTouchEvent(MotionEvent event);
```

When a user clicks, releases, moves, or does other interactive actions on the touchscreen, a touch input event is generated. This touch input event triggers the call to View.onTouchEvent. To allow users to process touchscreen input, you need to rewrite this function. The response code needs to be written in the function's body.

View.onTouchEvent has a parameter of type MotionEvent that defines the coordinate position of the touch point, event type, and so on of the MotionEvent class. The event types can be MotionEvent.ACTION_DOWN, MotionEvent.ACTION_MOVE, MotionEvent. ACTION_UP, or equivalent, as defined constants in the MotionEvent class. The constants represent interactive actions such as a touchscreen press, touchscreen move, touchscreen pop-up, and so on.

As discussed earlier, whenever the view needs to be redrawn, the View.onDraw function is called, so the drawing code needs to be put into the function. Most of the time, the system can automatically trigger redraw events; but because users design their own redraws, the system does not know when they need to be triggered. For example, perhaps a user updates the display content, but the location, size, and levels of the content are not changed; as a result, the system does not trigger the redraw event. In this situation, the user needs to call the class function postInvalidate or invalidate of the View class to proactively generate the redraw events. The function prototype is

```
void  View.invalidate(Rect dirty)
void  View.invalidate(int l, int t, int r, int b)
void  View.invalidate()
void  View.postInvalidate(int left, int top, int right, int bottom)
void  View.postInvalidate()
```

The postInvalidate and invalidate functions with no parameters redraw the entire view; the postInvalidate and invalidate functions with parameters redraw the designated area (or certain area) of the view. The difference between postInvalidate and invalidate with and without constants is that the first case requires an event loop until the next issue to produce the redraw event, whereas the second one immediately issues a redraw.

The following example illustrates the framework of drawing code that responds to touchscreen input. The interface of the application is shown in Figure 4-3.

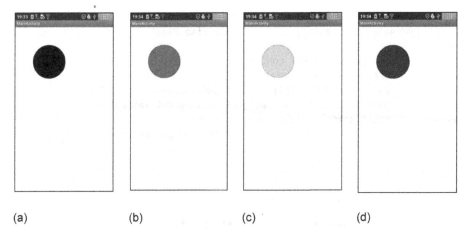

(a)   (b)   (c)   (d)

Figure 4-3. *The interface of a GuiExam input graphics framework that responds to the touchscreen*

The application starts in Figure 4-3(a). When the user clicks inside a circle (touches the screen within the circle area), the color of the circle changes: it cycles through black, red, green, and blue, as shown in Figure 4-3(a)-(d). If you click outside the circle, the circle does not change colors.

Using the same example as in the earlier section, modify the custom view class MyView.java as follows:

```
Line#        Source Code
1   package com.example.guiexam;
2
3   import android.view.View;
4   import android.graphics.Canvas;
5   import android.graphics.Paint;
6   import android.content.Context;
7
8   import android.graphics.Color;
9   import android.view.MotionEvent;
10  import java.lang.Math;

11  public class MyView extends View {
12      private float cx = 250;        // Default X Coordinate of Circle
13      private float cy = 250;        // Default Y Coordinate of Circle
14      private int radius = 120;      // Radius
15      private int colorArray[] = {Color.BLACK, Color.RED, Color.GREEN,
                                    Color.BLUE };
16  // Defines an array of colors
```

```
17    private int colorIdx = 0;     // Custom color subscript
      private Paint paint;          // Define Paint
18
19    public MyView(Context context) {
20        super(context);
21        paint = new Paint();        // Initialization paintbrush
22        paint.setAntiAlias(true); // Setting anti-aliasing
23        paint.setColor(colorArray[colorIdx]);
                                      // Set the pen color
  }


24
25   @Override
26   protected void onDraw(Canvas canvas) {
27       canvas.drawCircle(cx, cy, radius, paint);
  }


28
29    @Override
30    public boolean onTouchEvent(MotionEvent event) {
31        float px = event.getX();
32 // defined the touch point in the X, Y coordinates
33        float py = event.getY();
34        switch (event.getAction()) {
35        case MotionEvent.ACTION_DOWN:
36 // Touch  screen pressed
37 if (Math.abs(px-cx) < radius && Math.abs(py-cy) < radius){
38 // Touch location inside the circle
39     colorIdx = (colorIdx + 1) % colorArray.length;
40             paint.setColor(colorArray[colorIdx]);
41 // Set paintbrush color
42                     }
43                 postInvalidate();
  // Repaint
44               break;
45           case MotionEvent.ACTION_MOVE:
  // Screen touch and move
46               break;
47           case MotionEvent.ACTION_UP:
  // Screen touch unpressed
              break;
          }
          return true;
    }
  }
```

Lines 15 and 16 define an array of colors and color indices, and line 17 defines paintbrush variables. Lines 20–22 of the constructor function complete the initialization of the brush property settings. The reason you do not put the code for the paintbrush property set in View.Ondraw is to avoid repeated calculations for each redraw. The only work for the onDraw function is to display the circle.

In lines 28–46, you create the new touch input event response function onTouchEvent. In lines 30 and 32, you first get the X, Y coordinates of the touch point using the getX and getY functions of the MotionEvent class. Then you obtain the input action type through the getAction function of the MotionEvent class in line 34, followed by a case statement to complete the different input actions. The response to the action of pressing the touchscreen is in lines 37–43. You determine whether the touch point is within the circle in line 37. Then you modify the codes that set the colors and change the pen color in lines 39–40. You call the postInvalidate function notification to redraw in line 43 and provide it with the final finishing touch.

Multi-Touch Code Framework

Most Android devices support multi-touch touchscreens. The good news is that the Android system software also provides multi-touch support. This section covers the multi-touch code framework.

The touch event class MotionEvent has a getPointerCount() function that returns the current number of touch points on the screen. The function prototype is

```
final int MotionEvent.getPointerCount();
```

You can also use the getX and getY functions discussed earlier to obtain the coordinates of the touch point. The prototypes are as follows:

```
final float  MotionEvent.getX(int pointerIndex)
final float  MotionEvent.getX()
final float  MotionEvent.getY(int pointerIndex)
final float  MotionEvent.getY()
```

In the previous section, you got the coordinates of a single touch point using a function with no parameters. The getX/getY functions with parameters are used to get the position of the touch point in the multi-point touch situation, where the parameter pointerIndex is the index number for the touch point. This is an integer number starting at 0.

Here is an example to illustrate the multi-touch programming framework. This example is a two-point touch application that zooms a circle in and out. The application interface is shown in Figure 4-4.

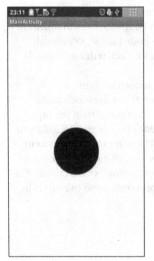 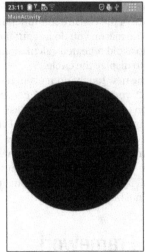 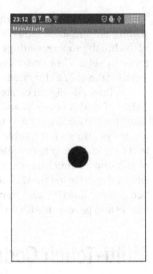

(a) Initial interface after the application starts

(b) Enlarged circle after a two-point touch zoom-in

(c) Downsized circle after two-point touch zoom-out

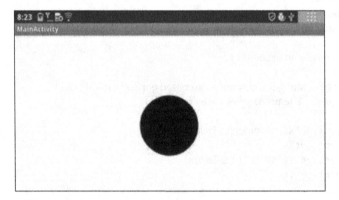

(d) Interface with the screen rotated 90 degrees

Figure 4-4. *The interface of the two-point touch zoom-in/zoom-out GuiExam graphic application*

The application's launch interface is shown in Figure 4-4(a). The circle is always at the center of the view, but the size of the circle (its radius) can be controlled by a two-point touch. The center is the center of the view, not the center of the activity or the center of the screen. The so-called two-point touchscreen means there are two touch points, or two fingers moving on the screen at the same time, either in an expand gesture where the circle becomes larger (b) or in squeeze gesture where the circle becomes smaller (c). The code is as follows:

```
Line#        Source Code
1  package com.example.guiexam;
2
3  import android.view.View;
4  import android.graphics.Canvas;
5  import android.graphics.Paint;
6  import android.content.Context;
7
8  import android.view.MotionEvent;
9  import java.lang.Math;

10 public class MyView extends View {
11    private static final int initRadius = 120; // initial value ofthe radius
12    private float cx;                      // X coordinate of the circle
13    private float cy;                      // Y coordinate of the circle
14    private int radius = initRadius;       // Set initial value of
                                              the radius
15    public float graphScale = 1;           // Set Scale factor for one
                                              two-point touch move
16    private float preInterPointDistance;   // Pre-distance of two touch
                                              points
17    private boolean bScreenPress = false;  // The sign of the screen being
                                              pressed down
18    private Paint paint;                   // Define paintbrush

19    public MyView(Context context) {
20      super(context);
21      paint = new Paint();                 // Initialize paintbrush
22      paint.setAntiAlias(true);            // Set Anti Alias
23 }

24    @Override
25    protected void onDraw(Canvas canvas) {
26    cx = canvas.getWidth()/2;              // Let circle center positioned
                                              at the screen of the screen
27    cy = canvas.getHeight()/2;
28      canvas.drawCircle(cx, cy, radius*graphScale, paint);
29 }
```

```
30      @Override
31      public boolean onTouchEvent(MotionEvent event) {
32          float px1, py1;          // Define the X,Y coordinates of 1st touch
                                         point
33          float px2, py2;          // Define the X,Y coordinates of 2nd touch
                                         point
34          float interPointDistance;    //distance between two  touch points
35          switch (event.getAction()) {
36          case MotionEvent.ACTION_DOWN:        // Screen touch pressed
37                                       break;
38          case MotionEvent.ACTION_MOVE:        // Screen touch move
39              if (event.getPointerCount() == 2 ) {
40                  px1 = event.getX(0);   //Get the X,Y coordinate of the
                                               first touch point
41                  py1 = event.getY(0);
42                  px2 = event.getX(1);          // Get the X,Y coordinate of
                                                      the second touch point
43                  py2 = event.getY(1);
44                  interPointDistance = (float) Math.sqrt((px6-px2)*(px6-
                        px2)+(py1 - py2)*(py1 - py2));
45                  if (!bScreenPress){
46                      bScreenPress = true;
47                      preInterPointDistance = interPointDistance;
48                  } else {
49                      graphScale = interPointDistance
                                        // preInterPointDistance;
50                      invalidate();   // Redraw graphics
51                  }
52              } else {
53                  bScreenPress = false;
54                  radius = (int)(radius * graphScale);
55 // One downsize/enlarge circle end. Record final scale factor
56              }
57              break;
58          case MotionEvent.ACTION_UP:          // Screen touch lift up
59              bScreenPress = false;
60              radius = (int)(radius * graphScale);
61 // One downsize/enlarge circle end. Record final scale factor
62              break;
63          }
64          return true;
        }
    }
```

This code defines a scaling factor graphScale for a two-point touch in line 15 and a variable preInterPointDistance in line 16 to record the distance between the two touch points. Line 17 defines the flag variable bScreenPress when the screen is pressed.

Lines 26 and 27 call getWidth and getHeight of the Canvas class in the onDraw function to get the view's width and height, and then allocate the center of the circle in the center of the view. The advantage of this step is that, when the screen rotates 90 degrees, the circle remains in the center of the view, as shown in Figure 4-4(d). The difference between these examples and the previous one is that this time the radius of the circle being drawn is equal to the radius of the circle multiplied by the scaling factor graphScale.

Lines 32–61 contain onDraw based on the modified example in the previous section. Lines 38–56 are the response code for a touch-move activity. Line 3 determines whether there are two touch points; if there are, you run code lines 40–51; otherwise, you run lines 53–54. You set the flag bScreenPress to false to indicate when the two touch points are first pressed, and then you record the final radius as equal to the current value of the radius multiplied by the scaling factor graphScale. You get the position coordinates of the two touch points in lines 40–43. Line 44 calculates the distance between the two touch points. Line 45 determines whether it is the first press; if it is, lines 46 and 47 run, and record the distance between the two touch points; otherwise, the code in lines 49–50 runs. Here you calculate the scaling factor based on the current distance between the points and the distance in the previous movement. After this, the graphic is redrawn.

To handle the location of the flag bScreenPress, you execute the response code of the screen touch-up activity in lines 58–60, which is similar to the non-two-point touch code in lines 53 and 54.

Responding to Keyboard Input

Most Android devices have a number of hardware buttons, such as Volume +, Volume -, Power, Home, Menu, Back, Search, and so on. Some Android devices are also equipped with keyboards. Keyboards, including the device's hardware buttons, are important input methods for Android applications. Keyboard input corresponds to keyboard events, named KeyEvent (also known as a *pressing key event*). In this section, you learn about the methods to respond to keyboard input.

In Android, both the Activity and View classes can receive pressed-key events. Key events trigger calls to the onKeyDown function of the Activity or View class. The function prototype is

```
boolean    Activity.onKeyDown(int keyCode, KeyEvent event);
boolean    View.onKeyDown(int keyCode, KeyEvent event);
```

The keyCode parameter is the index code of the key that is pressed. Each key in Android has a unique number, which is the keyCode. Some of the key codes were described in Table 1-1. The key event, KeyEvent, contains properties related to buttons, such as the frequency with which they are pressed. To handle key events, you need to override the onKeyDown function and add your own response-handling code.

Interestingly, although the Activity and View classes can receive key events, the view is often included in the activity. When the button is pressed, the event first sends external activity; that is, the activity receives the event sooner. The following example shows how you respond to the button press by rewriting the activity's onKeyDown function.

This example shows how to use the arrow keys to move the circle in the application. The application interface is shown in Figure 4-5.

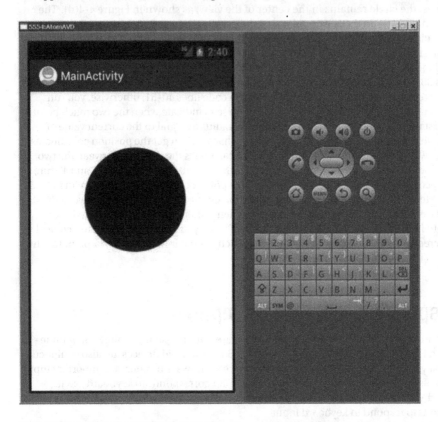

(a) Interface when the application starts

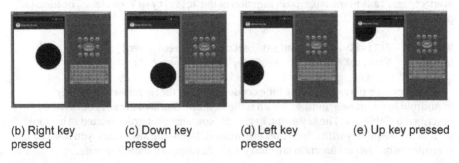

(b) Right key   (c) Down key   (d) Left key   (e) Up key pressed
pressed   pressed   pressed

Figure 4-5. *Using keys to control the movement of the circle in the application interface*

The Lenovo phone on which we are testing has no keypad, so we chose to run the application on a virtual machine. The virtual machine has Left, Down, Right, and Up keys to achieve these circle movements. The application startup interface is shown in Figure 4-5(a). Pressing the Left, Down, Right, or Up button makes the circle move in the corresponding direction. The interface examples are shown in Figure 4-5(b) through (e).

This application is based on the example, created at the beginning of this chapter (Figure 4-1) and modified per the following procedure:

4. Modify the source code of MyView.java as follows:

```
Line#        Source Code
1   package com.example.guiexam;
2
3   import android.view.View;
4   import android.graphics.Canvas;
5   import android.graphics.Paint;
6   import android.content.Context;
7   public class MyView extends View {
8       private float cx = 250;      // X coordinate of the circle
9       private float cy = 250;      // Y coordinate of the circle
10      private static final int radius = 120; // Radius of the circle
11      private Paint paint;                 // define paint brush
12      private static final int MOVESTEP = 10;    // the step
        length for pressing direction key

13      public MyView(Context context) {
14          super(context);
15          paint = new Paint();                 // Paint brush
            initialization
16          paint.setAntiAlias(true);            // Set Anti Alias
17      }

18      @Override
19      protected void onDraw(Canvas canvas) {
20          canvas.drawCircle(cx, cy, radius, paint);
21      }

22      ////// Self-define function:press key to move graphic
        (circle) //////
23      public void moveCircleByPressKey(int horizon, int
        vertical){
```

```
24      if (horizon < 0)                    // horizontal move
25          cx -= MOVESTEP;
26      else if (horizon > 0)
27          cx += MOVESTEP;
28      if (vertical < 0)
29          cy += MOVESTEP;                  // vertical move
30      else if (vertical > 0)
31          cy -= MOVESTEP;
32      postInvalidate();                    // note to repaint
33   }
34 }
```

In lines 23–33, you add a function to the view class to move the image (the circle) by pressing the horizon or vertical key. This function takes two arguments: horizon and vertical. If horizon is less than 0, you decrease the X coordinate value of the circle, and as a result, the circle moves to the left. If horizon is greater than 0, you increase the X coordinate value of the circle, which moves the circle to the right. You do a similar operation for the vertical parameters to move the circle up and down. Line 32 updates the graphics routine with new parameters and trigger the view to redraw.

5. Modify the source code of the main activity class MainActivity.java as follows:

```
Line#        Source Code
1   package com.example.guiexam;
2   import android.os.Bundle;
3   import android.app.Activity;
4   import android.view.Menu;
5   import android.view.KeyEvent;        // Key press event class

6   public class MainActivity extends Activity {
7       private MyView theView =null; // View object stored inside
                                            the variable

8       @Override
9       public void onCreate(Bundle savedInstanceState) {
10          super.onCreate(savedInstanceState);
11          theView = new MyView(this); // record the View class
                                            of the Activity
12          setContentView(theView);
13      }

14      @Override
15      public boolean onCreateOptionsMenu(Menu menu) {
16          getMenuInflater().inflate(R.menu.activity_main, menu);
17          return true;
18      }
```

```
19      @Override        // Key down response function
20      public boolean onKeyDown(int keyCode, KeyEvent event) {
21          int horizon = 0; int vertical = 0;
22          switch (keyCode)
23          {
24              case KeyEvent.KEYCODE_DPAD_LEFT:
25                  horizon = -1;
26                  break;
27              case KeyEvent.KEYCODE_DPAD_RIGHT:
28                  horizon = 1;
29                  break;
30              case KeyEvent.KEYCODE_DPAD_UP:
31                  vertical = 1;
32                  break;
33              case KeyEvent.KEYCODE_DPAD_DOWN:
34                  vertical = -1;
35                  break;
36              default:
37                  super.onKeyDown(keyCode, event);
38          }
39          if (!(horizon == 0 && vertical == 0))
40              theView.moveCircleByPressKey(horizon,vertical);
41          return true;
42      }
43 }
```

In this code, you want the Activity class to receive and respond to key-down events, so you overwrite the onKeyDown function in lines 19–42 with the button-response code. Although the response function for key buttons is located in the Activity class, the display updates are to be implemented in the view MyView class, so you must make the Activity class aware of its corresponding view object. To do so, you add a record-view object variable theView in line 7. In lines 11 and 12, you let theView record this object when constructing the view object.

In the key-down response function onKeyDown, you use a switchcase statement (lines 22–38) and take different actions according to the different keys. The function's keyCode parameter specifies the key number of the key that is pressed. For example, the code in lines 24–26 is the handling code for the Left key. It sets a horizontal flag to "left" and then calls the self-defined function moveCircleByPressKey of the view class to move the circle in lines 39 and 40. To allow other key-press-down events to be addressed, you call the system's default handler to deal with other keys in lines 36 and 37.

Dialog Boxes in Android

There are three different ways to use dialog boxes in Android, as discussed in this section.

Using an Activity's Dialog Theme

The Dialog class implements a simple floating window that can be created in an activity. By using a basic Dialog class, you can create a new instance and set its title and layout. Dialog themes can be applied to a normal activity to make it look similar to a dialog box.

In addition, the Activity class provides a convenient mechanism to create, save, and restore dialogs, such as onCreateDialog(int), onPrepareDialog(int, Dialog), showDialog(int), dismissDialog(int), and other functions. If you use these functions, the activity can return the Activity object that manages the dialog through the getOwnerActivity() method.

The following are specific instructions for using these functions.

onCreateDialog(int) Function

When you use this callback function, Android sets this activity as the owner of each dialog box, which automatically manages the state of each dialog box and anchors it to the activity. In this way, each dialog inherits the specific attributes of this activity. For example, when a dialog box is opened, the menu button displays the option menu defined for the activity. For example, you can use the volume keys to modify the audio stream that the activity uses.

showDialog(int) Function

When you want to display a dialog box, you call the showDialog(intid) method and pass an integer through this function call that uniquely identifies this dialog. When the dialog box is first requested, Android calls onCreateDialog(intid) from the activity. You should initialize this dialog box. This callback method is passed to the same ID that showDialog(intid) has. When you create the dialog box, the object is returned at the end of the activity.

onPrepareDialog(int, Dialog) Function

Before the dialog box is displayed, Android also calls the optional callback function onPrepareDialog(int id, Dialog). If you want the properties to be changed every time a dialog box is opened, you can define this method. Unlike the onCreateDialog(int) function, which can only be called the first time you open the dialog box, this method is called each time you open the dialog box. If you do not define onPrepareDialog(), then the dialog remains the same as the last time it was opened. The dialog box's ID and the dialog object created in onCreateDialog() can also be passed to the function by this method.

dismissDialog(int) Function

When you are ready to close the dialog box, you can call dismiss() through this dialog box method to eliminate it. If desired, you can also call dismissDialog(int id) method from the activity. If you want to use the onCreateDialog(int id) method to retain the state of your dialog box, then each time the dialog box is eliminated, the status of the object of this dialog box object is kept in the activity. If you decide that you no longer need this object or clear the state, then you should call removeDialog(intid). This removes any internal object references, and even if the dialog box is being displayed, it is eliminated.

Using a Specific Dialog Class

Android provides multiple classes that are expansions of the Dialog class, such as AlertDialog, .ProgressDialog, .and so on. Each class is designed to provide specific dialog box functions. The screen interface based on the Dialog class is created in all activities that then call the specific class. So it does not need to be registered in the manifest file, and its life cycle is controlled by the activity that calls the class.

Using Toast Reminders

Toasts are special, nonmodular, transient message dialog boxes, usually used in the broadcast receiver and backgroundservices, and used to prompt user events..

Dialog Box Example

Of the dialog box methods discussed, if it is measured by how the implementation of the function is done, the first function is the most powerful, followed by the second and third. In terms of the degree of sophistication of the implementation code, the third method is the simplest, and the first and the second are more complex.

The following example demonstrates the second method. See Android's help documentation and samples (in the samples directory located under the Android SDK installation directory) to learn more about the other implementation methods.

The specific dialog box class that this sample application uses is the Builder inner class of AlertDialog. When you press the Back button, a dialog box pops up, allowing you to decide whether to exit the application. The application interface is shown in Figure 4-6. Using the Android dialog box in this example will help you understand its usage.

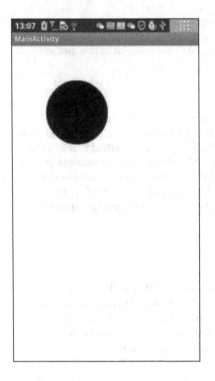

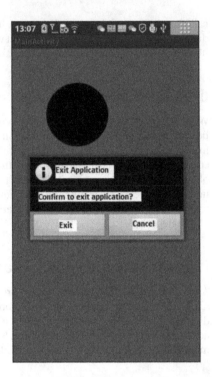

(a) Interface when the application starts, and after Cancel is pressed

(b) Interface after Return key is pressed

Figure 4-6. *The application interface with an Exit dialog box*

The application starts and displays the main activity interface, as shown in Figure 4-6(a). When you press the device's Back button, the Exit dialog box pops up, as shown in Figure 4-6(b). When you click the Exit button, the application exits, and the interface is also closed. When you click the Cancel button, the application returns to the previous screen, similar to Figure 4-6(a).

Modify the source code of the activity class MainActivity.java to read as follows:

```
Line#          Source Code
1  package com.example.guiexam;
2  import android.os.Bundle;
3  import android.app.Activity;
4  import android.view.Menu;
5  import android.view.KeyEvent;          // Key event class
6  import android.app.Dialog;             // Use Dialog class
```

124

```
7  import android.app.AlertDialog;         // Use AlertDialog class
8  import android.content.DialogInterface; // Use DialogInterface interface

9  public class MainActivity extends Activity {
10     private MyView theView =null;        // View objects stored inside
       the variable
11     private AlertDialog.Builder exitAppChooseDlg = null; // Exit App
       dialog box
12     private Dialog dlgExitApp = null;

13     @Override
14     public void onCreate(Bundle savedInstanceState) {
15         super.onCreate(savedInstanceState);
16         theView = new MyView(this); //View class of Record My Activity
17         setContentView(theView);

18         exitAppChooseDlg = new AlertDialog.Builder(this);
19 // Define  AlertDialog.Builder object
20         exitAppChooseDlg.setTitle("Exit Selection");
21 // Define the title of the dialog box
22         exitAppChooseDlg.setMessage("Confirm to exit application?");
22 // Define the display text of the dialog box
23         exitAppChooseDlg.setIcon(android.R.drawable.ic_dialog_info);
24 // Define the icon of the dialog box
25
26 // Set the leftmost button and click response class
27         exitAppChooseDlg.setPositiveButton("Exit", new DialogInterface.
           OnClickListener() {
28             public void onClick(DialogInterface dialog, int which) {
29                 dialog.dismiss();            // Close Dialog Box
                   /*MainActivity.*/finish();   // Exit (main) Activity
30                 System.exit(0);              // Exit Application
31             }
32         });
33
34 // Set the rightmost button and click response class
35         exitAppChooseDlg.setNegativeButton("Cancel",
           new DialogInterface.OnClickListener() {
36             public void onClick(DialogInterface dialog, int which)
               {
37                 dialog.cancel();        // Close dialog box
               }
38         });
39         dlgExitApp = exitAppChooseDlg.create();
40 // Create dialog box exit object
41     }
42
```

```
    @Override
43  public boolean onCreateOptionsMenu(Menu menu) {
44      getMenuInflater().inflate(R.menu.activity_main, menu);
45      return true;
46  }
47
48  @Override        //Key down response function
49  public boolean onKeyDown(int keyCode, KeyEvent event) {
50      int horizon = 0; int vertical = 0;
51      switch (keyCode)
52      {
53          case KeyEvent.KEYCODE_DPAD_LEFT:
54              horizon = -1;
55              break;
56          case KeyEvent.KEYCODE_DPAD_RIGHT:
57              horizon = 1;
58              break;
59          case KeyEvent.KEYCODE_DPAD_UP:
60              vertical = 1;
61              break;
62          case KeyEvent.KEYCODE_DPAD_DOWN:
63              vertical = -1;
64              break;
65          case KeyEvent.KEYCODE_BACK:
66              if (event.getRepeatCount() == 0) {
67                  dlgExitApp.show();
68  // Display AlertDialog.Builder dialog box
69              }
70              break;
71          default:
72              super.onKeyDown(keyCode, event);
        }
        if (!(horizon == 0 && vertical == 0))
            theView.moveCircleByPressKey(horizon,vertical);
        return true;
    }
}
```

Lines 11 and 12 define the AlertDialog.Builder class and its associated variable for the Dialog class in the Activity class. You modify the onCreate function code in lines 18–36 and define the code to prepare the dialog box. In line 18, you construct the AlertDialog.Builder class object; the prototype of this constructor function is

```
AlertDialog.Builder(Context context)
AlertDialog.Builder(Context context, int theme)
```

You use the first prototype in this example to pass the Activity object, which constructs the dialog box as the context of the constructor function. This is followed by setting the title display text, icons, and other attributes of the dialog box in lines 19 and 21.

The AlertDialog.Builder dialog box can take up to three buttons: left, middle, and right. They are set up by the setPositiveButton, setNeutralButton, and setNegativeButton functions, respectively. You can specify how many dialog box buttons you need. This example uses two buttons: left and right.

Lines 23-29 set the left button of the dialog box and click-response code. The prototype of the setPositiveButton function of the AlertDialog.Builder class is

```
AlertDialog.Builder  setPositiveButton(int textId, DialogInterface.
OnClickListener listener)
AlertDialog.Builder  setPositiveButton(CharSequence text, DialogInterface.
OnClickListener listener)
```

You use a second prototype in the example, where the first parameter is text displayed by the button, and the second parameter is the interface object of the click response.

In line 25, you first call the dismissal or cancel function of the DialogInterface class to close the dialog box. DialogInterface is the operating interface of the dialog class (AlertDialog, Dialog, and so on). You use the dismiss function to close the dialog box in line 25 and use a cancel function to close the dialog box in line 33.

Lines 26-27 close the activity and application, as described in the section "Exit Activities and Application." in Chapter 2, Figure 2-16. Interestingly, the internal class DialogInterface.OnClickListener uses a member function of the non-dot external class MainActivity and does not need to add the prefix in front of "class name."

You set the dialog box for the right button and click-response code in lines 36-35. The click-response code is relatively simple, using the cancel function of the DialogInterface class to close the dialog box in line 33.

Finally, line 36 calls the create function of the AlertDialog.Builder class to create the exit dialog box object dlgExitApp. The function returns an AlertDialog object, and its prototype is

```
AlertDialog  create()
```

Because AlertDialog is derived from the Dialog class, the return value can be assigned to the Dialog variable.

You add the Back key response code for the OnKeyDown response function on lines 60-64. The code is relatively simple: you determine whether duplicate keys are pressed on line 61, and then you call the show function of the Dialog class to display a dialog box.

Application Property Settings

In Android device, there are two difference places where you can find out the information about the applications installed. One is the menu list (the interface after you press the setting button), the other is by going to the Settings ➤ Applications ➤ Manage Applications ➤ Downloaded menu item. See Figure 4-7:

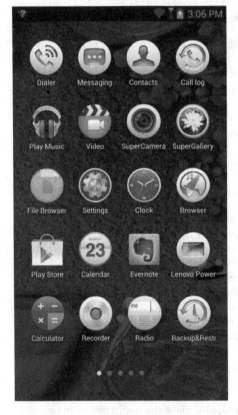

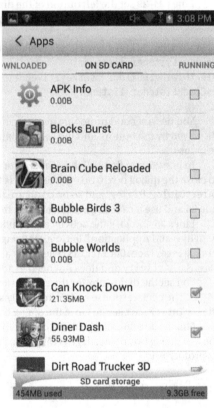

(a) Menu list on the target device

(b) Application settings on the target device

Figure 4-7. *The difference of Menulist and Application Setting display on target device*

So far, almost all the examples have been based on the code framework of two applications: GuiExam and HelloAndroid. But it is difficult to distinguish between them in the menu on the target device. These applications are indistinguishable in the menu list because you used the default settings instead of applying their own property settings. This section shows you how to apply property settings.

Figure 4-8 shows the applications setting interface before and after applying property settings.

(a) The icon and text of the original application on the menu list of the target device

(b) The icon and text of the application after applying property settings

Figure 4-8. *The application on the target device before and after applying property setting*

This example uses the GuiExam application to show the steps for changing the application settings:

1. Modify the icon of the application in the menu on the target machine. Based on the ic_launcher.png file size under the application res\drawable-XXX directory (where XXX represents different resolutions—for example, drawable-hdpi represents the directory for high-resolution images), edit your image file, and name it ic_launcher.png.

The common screen resolutions for Android devices and the directories where application icon files are stored are shown in Table 4-2.

Table 4-2. *Common Android Device Screen Resolutions and the Directories Containing Application Icon Sizes*

Directory Name	Size	Description
drawable-ldpi	36 × 36 dpi	Low-resolution screen
drawable-mdpi	48 × 48 dpi	Medium-resolution screen
drawable-hdpi	72 × 72 dpi	High-resolution screen
drawable-xhdpi	96 × 96 dpi	Super-high-resolution screen
drawable-xxhdpi	144 × 144 dpi	Extra-extra-high-resolution screen

2. Put the custom picture file in the corresponding directory res\drawable-XXX, and replace the original file. For example, for the high-resolution screen application, replace the file ic_launcher.png in res\drawable-xhdpi with your own, as shown in Figure 4-9.

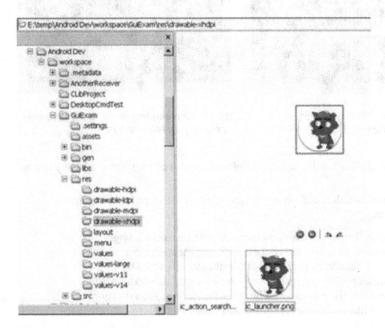

Figure 4-9. *Replacing the application icon*

3. Modify the application's menu text annotation on the target machine.

Open the Package Explorer pane of the \res\values\strings.xml file. The title_ activity_my_main string value is set to a custom string (in this case, "GUI examples"), as shown in Figure 4-10.

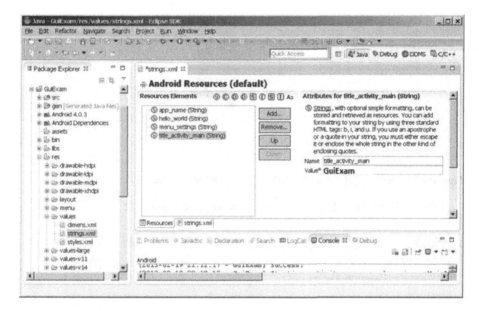

Figure 4-10. *Modifying the icon text of the application*

After completing these modifications, you can see that the target application's menu item's icon and text label have changed.

Note step 1 can also be implemented by another method that can generate its own set of icons when the application is created. The procedure is as follows:

1. In the Configure Launcher Icon dialog box, click the Image button, and then click the Browse button to the right of Image File.

2. Select the picture file as the application icon (in this case, graywolf.png) in the Open dialog box, as shown in Figure 4-11.

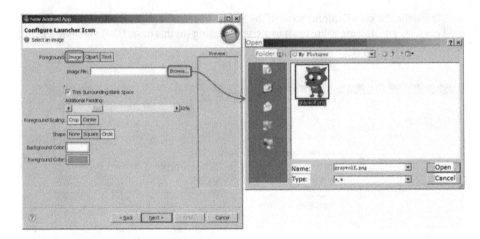

Figure 4-11. *Selecting the icon file when generating the application*

The Configure Launcher Icon dialog box is shown in Figure 4-12.

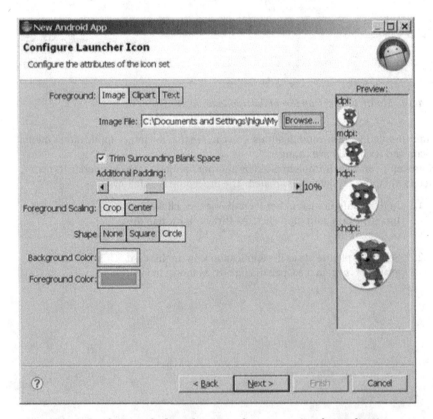

Figure 4-12. *Configuring the launcher icon when generating the application*

In other words, Eclipse can, based on the user-specified image file, automatically generate the various ic_launcher.png files with the appropriate dimensions in the res\drawable-XXX directory. This eliminates the need to manually edit the images.

In this last chapter covering Android GUI design, you are introduced to the basic framework of drawings in the view, the concept of how the drawing Framework responds to touch screen input, and how to control the display of the view as well as the multi-touch code framework. You use an example that illustrates the multi-touch programming framework and keyboard input response. You learn the methods to respond to keyboard input and hardware buttons that are available on Android devices, such as Volume +, Volume -, Power, Home, Menu, Back, Search, and so on. You are introduced to the three different dialog boxes for Android, which include the activity dialog theme, a specific class dialog, and Toast reminder. At the end of the chapter, you learn how to change the application property settings.

Index

■ T, U, V, W, X, Y, Z